WINTER GARDENS

CÉDRIC POLLET

WINTER GARDENS

reinventing a season

FRANCES
LINCOLN

To my father and mother, for everything they gave me and taught me...

CONTENTS

The white stems of *Rubus cockburnianus*
'Goldenvale' undulate beneath a fiery *Cornus alba*
'Sibirica'. In the foreground *Cornus sanguinea*
'Midwinter Fire' sets the garden ablaze.
(WISLEY, ENGLAND)

INTRODUCTION

Finding the subject of a book and then giving it life by publishing it arises first and foremost from the author's desire to share with readers a real passion born from wonderful stories and unforgettable encounters. For my first book, *Bark, An Intimate Look at the World's Trees,* it was an age-old English oak I encountered in 1999 that opened my eyes.

For this book, *Winter Gardens, Reinventing a Season,* my starting point wasn't a venerable tree but rather a person who loves trees, Christian Peyron, and my discovery in 2007 of his incredible garden, the Jardin du Bois Marquis. On my first visit there I was like a child discovering their presents beneath the Christmas tree. My eyes sparkled, drawn irresistibly by the richness of all the barks in his collection of trees. After my initial excitement I began to observe the garden more carefully. This was the moment when I fell in love at first sight with an incredible group of snakebark maples standing in front of a sea of the fiery stems of red dogwoods. The spectacle was almost unreal.

Since an image is often very much more effective than long descriptions, if I was to produce a book I needed to find other winter scenes just as colourful and spectacular. In Christian's opinion, England was a must; there, in 2009, I discovered a model for winter gardens, the Sir Harold Hillier Gardens. Christian also introduced me to other bark enthusiasts, in particular his friend Jean-Louis Dantec and the nurseryman Jean-Pierre Hennebelle, who in turn helped me a lot in my research.

In winter it's tempting to stay inside beside a blazing fire. Rain, damp, cold, fog and the lack of light discourage us from putting on our boots and going out. But frost and snow are not the only magic wands that you can count on to beautify your garden at this time of year. Nor do gardeners need to resign themselves to waiting for the first great spring flowering that marks nature's reawakening. The palette of winter plants is so rich that, provided the choice of species has been carefully thought out, the garden can be transformed in this season into a fairyland of luminous colours and subtle scents.

Apart from visual originality and the element of surprise, I find the simplicity and effectiveness of such winter gardens deeply moving. It is not necessary to have a multiplicity of plants. A few grouped plantings, limited to three or four different species that are repeated several times, create the best effect. Better still, most of these plants, chosen for their handsome bark and coloured stems, show their full effect from an early age and offer notable autumn foliage. All that remains now is for you to add some spring- and summer-flowering species to make your composition attractive throughout the year.

Today people are waking up to the colour and beauty of winter gardens, and many public parks and gardens encourage visitors to venture out in the cold by planting trees and shrubs that are at their peak of interest in mid-winter.

I have felt a strong attachment to England ever since I did part of my studies there. Together with France, this country is in the vanguard as regards winter gardens. It was thus natural to take these two countries as a model for further study. In fact, winter gardens are limited to regions with a temperate climate. This is why, apart from a few rare exceptions (eucalyptus, arbutus), the Mediterranean flora does not figure in this book.

The first two sections of the book illustrate the most beautiful winter garden scenes to be found in France and the United Kingdom. They offer a great many seductive ideas to spur you to make your gardens colourful, reinventing the winter season that is so often neglected. Four exceptional gardens stand out in this section — four delights that pay homage to four

With well-chosen plants the winter garden can be equally
spectacular throughout the autumn.

(MARKS HALL GARDENS & ARBORETUM, ENGLAND)

My encounter in 2007 with this colourful planting of snakebark maples and red dogwoods was a revelation.

(JARDIN DU BOIS MARQUIS, FRANCE)

passionate men who devoted their lives to plants, thus contributing to the development of horticulture in their countries.

The third and final section of the book presents plants of unbeatable value that will enable you to create a successful winter garden. The species proposed are far from constituting an exhaustive list, but they will provide you with sufficient key plants to fill your garden with magical colour during this season. My aim is to focus on the multicoloured stems and bark that are too often ignored in gardening literature. Indeed, in books on winter gardens priority is always given to fragrant flowers, colourful fruits or unusual evergreen foliage. I have thus wished to go against this trend by giving pride of place to bark in these spectacular wintry compositions.

This book is thus not a practical guide to the important activities that need to be carried out during the winter (pruning, protecting, improving the soil). It is above all an act of homage that I wish to pay to all those visionary gardeners who have inspired me so much over the past few years. The book is also addressed to everyone who loves plants or is passionate about gardens, as well as to landscape professionals. Winter is a season full of colour and light that rivals the exuberance of spring and the flamboyance of autumn. It is also one of gentleness and beauty which I hope this book captures and, speaking to your poetic soul, provides a refuge from the season's rigours.

THE WINTER GARDEN: A NEW STYLE OF GARDENING

The term "winter garden" appeared for the first time in England at the beginning of the 19th century but its meaning was very different from what we understand by the words today. During the Victorian age many towns built amazing glass palaces where people could amuse themselves, dance or listen to music. These popular venues became exotic glasshouses, veritable urban Gardens of Eden to be visited in the depths of winter, particularly at spa towns such as Bath, Brighton or Harrogate. The concept of a "winter garden" had been born. After the First World War these botanical paradises rapidly disappeared, their maintenance having become more and more of a burden.

The idea of using bark for purely ornamental purposes to brighten up a garden during the monotony of winter took some time to be recognized as a distinct style. Its early manifestations were all inspired by the same idea: the creation of a place that would remain attractive throughout the year and especially in winter. The great landscape designers and gardeners of those early days had too limited a choice of plants with beautiful bark to allow them to conceive of a winter garden worthy of the name. The three principal genera with decorative bark – *Betula* (birch), *Acer* (maple) and *Prunus* (cherry) – were introduced late into Europe. Some species, mainly American (the Pennsylvania maple, the black birch and the paper birch), had arrived by 1750. Yet it was not until the end of the 19th and beginning of the 20th centuries that the available range of species with ornamental bark was enriched, mostly with plants that came from China. The plants discovered by the French botanist Père David and by the British explorers and botanists Hooker and Wilson were crucial to this progress.

Nevertheless, we see some signs of interest in coloured bark during the 1860s, in various horticultural publications by the English nurseryman William Paul. In 1908 Gertrude Jekyll, one of the most influential landscape designers of the time, published a book on colour in the garden (*Colour Schemes for the Flower Garden*), her favourite subject. In Chapter 17, 'Planting for Winter Colour', she notes the importance of colourful bark and stems to provide vitality in winter. She pays homage to Lord Somers, a pioneer who more than 50 years earlier had had the idea of bringing colour to the woods around his home, Eastnor Castle, north of Bristol, with the luminous, multicoloured stems of various willows and dogwoods.

Then the taste for ornamental bark disappeared. It wasn't until the end of the Second World War that people rediscovered an enthusiasm for gardening. From then on, various horticultural specialists became increasingly interested in winter colour and in the visual potential that bark could bring to the garden. Stanley Whitehead (*The Winter Garden*, 1948) and Graham Stuart Thomas (*Colour in the Winter Garden*, 1957) were among the first authors to write entire books on this subject.

The idea in 1951 of devoting a space specifically to winter can be credited to John Gilmour, then Director of the Cambridge University Botanic Garden. His first arrangement, very formal in style, involved a few square and rectangular beds planted solely with species that offered ornamental interest in winter. The aim was to show off these plants individually in order to study them, without really integrating them into a landscape design.

Only in the early 1960s did the first real creations of this new style of garden emerge. At that time Alan Bloom's nursery was known throughout the world for its collections of perennials. But his son, Adrian Bloom, soon developed a unique range of conifers with very varied habits, needles and colours. In 1962, in response to the bleak winter landscape in

Foggy Bottom in March 1989: more than 20 years after its
creation, the very first winter landscape garden looks good with
its carpets of heathers, multicoloured dwarf conifers and birches.
(BRESSINGHAM GARDENS, ENGLAND)

the perennial garden inherited from his father, he created what was without doubt one of
the very first winter gardens in garden history. It consisted mainly of slow-growing dwarf
conifers, accompanied by a birch and a few winter flowers. In 1967 he decided to go further
and created another garden around his house, Foggy Bottom. He started his plantings with
a predominance of conifers and heathers, interspersed with a few witch hazels, a golden-
white dogwood and a three-trunked knobbly birch. Encouraged by this project, in 1972 he
wrote his first reference work on conifers, *Conifers for Your Garden*. In the mid-1970s Adrian
Bloom improved his garden by adding numerous remarkable trees and shrubs that were of
ornamental interest throughout the year. It was only around 1980 that he completed the
composition of his winter landscape with simple and striking plants such as grasses. In 1993
he brought together all he had learned about planting for winter in his best-selling book
Winter Garden Glory.

At the same time, other specialist nurserymen were proposing new clones of trees that
were of interest for their striking and varied bark. A passion for winter gardens ensued.

In Engand the first institution to experiment with this new concept was the Department
of Botany at the University of Cambridge. In 1978 Peter Orriss, then Director of the Garden,
decided with his team to improve the experimental plantings of 1951. Inspired by Adrian
Bloom and drawing on the lessons of the past, he created a new, original space devoted to
winter, this time in a more informal and landscaped style, which rapidly became a model for
other gardeners. The great English gardens then followed suit. These historic creations live
on at Wakehurst Place (1986), Rosemoor, the Sir Harold Hillier Gardens and Anglesey Abbey
(1996), Marks Hall Gardens & Arboretum (2000), Wisley (2002), once again with Bloom in
his Bressingham Gardens (2003), at Harlow Carr (2006), the Savill Garden (2008) and even at
Dunham Massey (2009), to cite only the most emblematic winter gardens in the UK.

Parallel to this, in France the idea that bark was important in a garden first appeared in
a small village in Normandy, Varengeville-sur-Mer. Here in 1957 Princess Greta Sturdza, a
leading figure in the world of horticulture and gardens, created her own Eden, Le Vasterival.
Her aim from the beginning was to design a garden for all four seasons, making particular use
of plants with ornamental interest in winter. Starting at the end of the 1960s, she planted the
first species whose bark she fell in love with: the Tibetan cherry, the cinnamon maple and Père
David's maple.

As Honorary President of the International Dendrology Society she was in regular contact
with eminent members of this renowned association, all of them keenly interested in plants

TOP: In their natural environment trees sometimes grow very close together. In spite of their proximity, these *Populus tremuloides* reach a normal height.

(ASPEN FOREST, COLORADO, UNITED STATES)

ABOVE: Having observed the way trees grow in the wild, in 1983 Jean-Pierre Hennebelle created a unique copse where the striking trunks of birches, maples and cherries brush lightly against each other without ill effects.

(HENNEBELLE NURSERY, FRANCE)

with fine bark and a winter flowering period. Her numerous exchanges with Prince Wolkonsky (Jardins de Kerdalo, Britanny), Bernard and Brigitte de La Rochefoucauld (Arboretum des Grandes Bruyères, Loiret), Sir Harold Hillier (the Sir Harold Hillier Gardens, England), Viscount Philippe de Spoelberch (Arboretum de Wespelaar, Belgium), and Baroness Jelena de Belder and her husband (Domaine d'Hemelrijk, Belgium) allowed her to unearth some real treasures. Thus a great many rare species or cultivars of birch, snakebark maple, cherries, Chilean myrtle, stewartias and clethras were progressively introduced into Le Vasterival for the beauty of their bark.

At about the same time, in 1959, Jean-Pierre Hennebelle created his nursery garden specializing in exceptional plants at Boubers-sur-Canche, in the Pas-de-Calais region. In 1976, he decided to travel to England to the renowned Sir Harold Hillier Gardens in order to enrich his collection of trees with interesting bark for the benefit of his clients in Normandy. Two years later he met Princess Sturdza and a great friendship began.

In 1979, breaking all horticultural rules, he was the first person to create a dense planting consisting entirely of trees with ornamental bark. He drew his inspiration from nature and from his forest walks. This tight planting, on an area of barely a few square yards, included two Himalayan white birches, one 'Princesse Sturdza' birch cultivar, a Manchurian cherry, two varieties of snakebark maple and a yellowwood ash. The French winter garden had borne its first fruits. Jean-Pierre Hennebelle gave priority to the simplicity and visual impact of bark, in contrast to the more profuse planting of the classic British winter garden.

A few years later, in 1983, he created a second, even denser planting, richer and ultimately more complete, which can still be admired behind his nursery. His aim was to show that it is possible to achieve a landscape, on a limited area and requiring very little maintenance, as ornamental as if nature herself had painted it.

Patrick Garçonnet, one of Hennebelle's faithful clients, was seduced by the brilliant whiteness of his Himalayan birch. At the end of the 1990s this bark enthusiast decided to create in turn his own winter garden, La Pommeraie, at Saint-Nicolas-d'Aliermont (in the Seine-Maritime region). Inspired by the planting that had so impressed him at the Hennebelle nursery, he developed his own garden around this winter theme.

During this time, Princess Sturdza was constantly continuing to gather enthusiasts around her, infecting them with her own passion for bark, in particular her great friend and neighbour Jean-Louis Dantec. On one of his many visits to Le Vasterival in 1989, Dantec was struck by the bark of a stewartia, a revelation which had a considerable influence on the creation of his own garden, L'Étang de Launay. With taste, delicacy and simplicity, but also with fierce passion, he collected among other things the trees with beautiful bark that he displays in his garden better than anyone else. In winter the play of colours he has created is spectacular, although it is just as impressive in other seasons.

In this same corner of Normandy, the birthplace of French winter gardens, Martine Lemonnier, a friend of Princess Sturdza, also uses trees with ornamental bark in her Jardins de Bellevue at Beaumont-le-Hareng. However, she places more emphasis on winter-flowering species such as witch hazels and especially hellebores, on which she has become a great specialist. These three passionate gardeners, the principal members of the very private club 'Fous de Jardins' ('Mad About Gardens') regularly share their research and discoveries and exchange plants to enrich their gardens, especially in winter.

Far away from all this excitement in Normandy, a small village near Lyon, Vernioz, was home to another pioneer just as passionate about bark: Christian Peyron and his Jardin du Bois

Set among colourful heathers and conifers, *Acer grosseri* var. *hersii*,
Betula papyrifera var. *commutata*, *Betula utilis* var. *jacquemontii*
'Jermyns' and *Betula* 'Hergest' were among the first plants with
ornamental bark used by Christian Peyron in the early 1980s in
his Jardin du Bois Marquis.

Marquis. When in 1980 he happened to come across a snakebark maple in a neighbourhood
nursery, it was a true revelation to him. This discovery was to have a strong influence on his
vision of his garden, so that from then on trees with attractive bark played the leading role in
his plantings. He began to create his winter garden, without a doubt the first in France worthy
of the name, by harmoniously associating different varieties of birch and snakebark maples with
coloured conifers and heathers.

Since Christian was not able to find in France all the rare plants he coveted, he decided
to learn how to graft them and set off to England to collect his own scions. This was the only
way for him to identify the best mother plants and thus to be sure of obtaining clones with the
finest bark possible. On his return he stopped at the famous nursery of Jean-Pierre Hennebelle
to stock up on special plants and exchange new discoveries.

With the enlargement of his garden in 1991, his collection of trees with ornamental
bark expanded significantly and now offers a unique and enchanting winter spectacle. Claude
Bellion of the Minier nurseries and his successor Jean-Noël Nivelle have played a major part
in the enrichment of French winter gardens. At the end of the 1990s they gave to the leading
bark enthusiasts many newly-introduced plants which they wanted to trial. Thanks to them,
Christian was able to meet the group of enthusiastic gardeners from Normandy. The very small
circle of French pioneers with a passion for bark and winter gardens was now complete.

WINTER GARDENS
FOUR FAVOURITES

L'ÉTANG
DE LAUNAY

Perched on the cliffs of Varengeville-sur-Mer in the Seine-Maritime region of France, L'Étang de Launay is a remarkable private garden covering almost 15 acres. It was created entirely by its owner, Jean-Louis Dantec, a lover of rare plants. Starting in 1990, this passionate gardener carried out titanic terracing work for 17 years. The gently undulating land was transformed into an idyllic garden, embellished with several large ponds. The soil of these former pastures is heavy and slightly acid, while the mild climate enjoys a significant level of rainfall – ideal conditions for the thousands of unusual species that grow harmoniously side by side and light up this paradise through all four seasons.

Thanks to Dantec's initial desire to create a sense of airy spaciousness and his use of a pruning technique that opens up the trees, the garden is full of light and exposed to the weak Normandy sun.

Strongly influenced by his friend and neighbour Princess Greta Sturdza (Le Vasterival), since 1989 he has had an overwhelming passion for trees with ornamental bark which he displays magnificently. He likes to combine them with hydrangeas, dogwoods, grasses and shrubs that bear flowers or fruits in winter (witch hazels, heathers, skimmias), as well as plants with striking evergreen foliage (rhododendrons, conifers). His compositions, specially designed to light up winter with blazing colour, are simple but nevertheless spectacular and highly effective.

The most representative collections at L'Étang de Launay are those of the genera *Betula*, *Acer*, *Prunus* and *Stewartia* but also *Magnolia*, *Hydrangea* and *Rhododendron*. They allow a perfect transition between the seasons.

Perched on its mossy promontory, *Betula utilis* var. *jacquemontii* dominates the pond. Its white bark contrasts with the conifers around it (*Chamaecyparis lawsoniana* 'Wissel's Saguaro', *Pinus mugo* etc).

TOP: Hydrangeas go extremely well with beautiful bark. At the entrance to L'Étang de Launay, the very floriferous *Hydrangea macrophylla* cultivars 'Tokyo Delight' and 'Vicomtesse de Vibraye' provide massed colour from summer until the first frosts.
ABOVE: In winter, the straw-yellow of the dry flower heads changes the dominant colour of this part of the garden.

In the absence of trees with coloured bark, the only way to make winter a delight is to find the right balance between deciduous and evergreen plants. During this season, the cloud-pruned shape of *Pinus sylvestris* 'Watereri' and the balls of *Taxus baccata* show better among bare trees. The wonderful *Edgeworthia chrysantha* 'Grandiflora' brings a floral touch which perfumes the path and lights up the garden.

The three multi-trunked specimens of *Betula utilis* var. *jacquemontii* are the principal feature of this planting. Around them are other key trees which ensure a smooth transition between the seasons: *Cornus controversa* 'Variegata', majestic with its spreading habit and pale green shoots in spring, *Taxodium distichum* 'Pendens' which turns a blazing red in autumn, and in the foreground *Acer palmatum* 'Sango-kaku' which becomes a ball of fire in winter.

All delicacy and poetry, the exuberant flowering of magnolias and ornamental cherries helps the garden to emerge gently from winter. Their pastel-coloured blossoms harmonize perfectly with the white trunks of the birches. Monsieur Dantec's favourite *Prunus* cultivars are 'The Bride', 'Collingwood Ingram' and 'Tai Haku'. Among magnolias, 'Leonard Messel' and 'J.C. Williams' are two of the cultivars he likes best.

The colour of bark changes according to the season.

TOP AND RIGHT: In summer *Acer tegmentosum* is already covered in a fine white skin.
This bloom lends it a blueish appearance which goes perfectly with the flowers of
Hydrangea serrata 'Verlee'. The *Prunus serrula* 'Jarro' in the centre has more of an orange
tint in this season. ABOVE: One has to wait until autumn and especially winter to admire
the coloured wood of *Cornus sanguinea* 'Winter Flame' and *Cornus alba* 'Westonbirt'.

When you are making your first plantings, don't hesitate to add volume quickly
by using fast-growing plants that change colour over the seasons.

ABOVE: Grasses such as the magnificent *Miscanthus sinensis* 'Gracillimus' rapidly
fill up space. Planted beneath a *Prunus maackii*, *Microbiota decussata* is an excellent
groundcover which takes on a bronze hue in winter.

It is always interesting to repeat the same colour at different levels of the planting.
TOP: *Cornus sanguinea* 'Winter Flame' on the left forms a handsome orange diagonal with
Prunus maackii in the centre and *Acer palmatum* 'Bi Hoo' in the foreground.
ABOVE: In early spring the white flowers of *Erica arborea* var. *alpina* × *veitchii* in the
foreground echo wonderfully those of *Magnolia stellata* 'Royal Star' in the centre.

Whatever the season, *Acer palmatum* 'Sango-kaku' is guaranteed to provide a spectacle.

TOP: In autumn its foliage has an intense colour. ABOVE: At the tips of its branches, the rosy new shoots remain very luminous all through the winter. The *Pinus sylvestris* and *Cryptomeria japonica* 'Elegans' that surround it show it off even more. *Cornus sanguinea* 'Winter Flame' stand like flamboyant sentinels in front of *Rhododendron yakushimanum* 'Koichiro Wada'.

RIGHT: In early spring, beneath the *Acer* 'Sango-kaku' the orange-red buds of *Edgeworthia chrysantha* 'Red Dragon' have waited all winter to burst open, like the dazzling white flowers of *Magnolia stellata*. The rhododendrons will then take up the baton while *Hydrangea paniculata* 'Early Sensation' will bring this magical scene to a close.

All of a sudden time stands still at L'Étang de Launay. Plants
succeed one another in a natural picture of almost insolent beauty.
TOP: In autumn *Acer palmatum* 'Jean-Louis Dantec' blazes and the two *Taxodium
ascendens* 'Nutans' continue to stoke the fire. ABOVE: Once the blaze is over, the
decorative qualities of *Betula nigra* (Hennebelle selection) and of *Prunus* 'Shirofugen'
leaning over the pond are elegantly reflected in the water throughout the winter.

The grand landscape all around the pond creates an incredible sense of serenity.
If there is a pond in the garden, winter will always be a magical season. The superb
Pinus parviflora 'Tempelhof' in the foreground and the conifers in the background
form a perfect frame for this idyllic picture. The water becomes a mirror, reflecting
the coloured barks of bamboos, willows, birches and dogwoods.

THE JARDIN DU BOIS MARQUIS

In the Rhone valley, about 25 miles south of Lyon, the village of Vernioz is home to a small jewel whose creator, Christian Peyron, is truly passionate about plants. Having fallen under the spell of *Acer pseudoplatanus* 'Brillantissimum', whose leaves start off pink in spring, and *Acer davidii* with its green bark streaked with white, he began gardening in the 1980s.

With no fences or hedges to mark its boundaries, he wanted to turn Bois Marquis into a magical space, freely accessible to everyone, where the enchantment would be permanent all year long. He has succeeded wonderfully well in this venture, especially in autumn and winter when people come from far afield to admire this festival of colour. Around the ponds, which are home to ornamental ducks, the other objects of his love, *Nyssa*, *Liquidambar* and some *Taxodium* species, set the garden aflame. The spectacle continues with the trees with multicoloured bark, his collection of which is by now the richest in France.

Christian Peyron was without doubt the first person in France to design a landscape specifically for winter, judiciously combining different varieties of birches with carpets of heather and coloured evergreens, such as various dwarf conifers.

Today his collections of *Betula*, *Acer*, *Prunus*, *Arbutus*, *Cornus*, bamboos, conifers, *Malus* and *Quercus* are spread over 5 of the 27 acres of the property. Although he never ceases to introduce horticultural novelties, usually to trial them, he does not do so solely in the spirit of a collector. He always gives priority to the aesthetic and striking qualities of a plant and to the overall harmony of the garden.

The purple of *Acer pectinatum* 'Sirene', the red of *Acer* × *conspicuum* 'Phoenix' and the yellowish-green of *Acer davidii* × *rufinerve* 'Albolimbatum' offer a fine example of the rich colour palette of the snakebark maples.

There is nothing like a mantle of snow to provide a wonderful contrast with the predominant red of this winter composition. After the autumnal blaze of *Euonymus alatus* and then the falling of its leaves, *Cornus sanguinea* 'Winter Flame' is fiery beneath maples. In the background *Acer pensylvanicum* 'Erythrocladum' takes on an orange-red colour while *Acer × conspicuum* 'Phoenix', in the front, acquires pinkish-red tones with the first cold weather.

Compose plantings with contrasting barks to show off your most beautiful specimens.
TOP: The vigorous, slightly violet-blue stems of *Acer negundo* var. *violaceum* stand out
perfectly against the orange background of *Cornus sanguinea* 'Winter Flame'.
ABOVE AND RIGHT: The chalky trunks of the rare *Betula* 'Fetisowii' contrast with the
shiny mahogany-coloured branchs of *Prunus serrula*.

In a landscape consisting only of deciduous species, the picture
rapidly becomes sad and monotonous once autumn is over.
ABOVE: To set the scene for trees with coloured bark it is essential
to include evergreens offering a wide range of colours, for example
heathers or conifers such as the grey-blue *Picea pungens* 'Glauca
Globosa' or *Pinus strobus* 'Nana' which has a light green centre.

TOP: Dogwoods combine the splendour of their foliage with the brilliance of their coloured stems. In autumn *Cornus alba* 'Westonbirt' opens the ball in its rosy-red gown.
ABOVE: Once its leaves have fallen, it displays its bright red stems for almost six months beneath *Acer davidii* 'Serpentine'. Three evergreens add rhythm to the scene: the small golden conifer *Calocedrus decurrens* 'Berrima Gold', the pale green bamboo *Phyllostachys aurea* 'Holochrysa' and the dark green column of *Pinus nigra* 'Fastigiata'.

Don't forget ornamental apple trees to give colour to your plantings. They are attractive in spring and autumn for their exuberant flowering and the small apples that sometimes remain on the tree throughout the winter. In the mist the golden *Malus transitoria* and the glowing *Malus* 'Donald Wyman' vie with the colourful stems of the *Acer palmatum* cultivars in the foreground, red in 'Eddisbury' and orange-yellow in 'Bi Hoo'.

You can also bring into play all the dry flower heads and fruits that remain on plants throughout the winter. TOP: The sparkling stems of *Cornus sanguinea* 'Winter Flame' make an excellent contrast with the dried black flower heads of *Phlomis russeliana*. ABOVE: The slightest ray of sun makes the small decorative apples of *Malus* 'Nicolas Hennebelle' glow. RIGHT: The pearly plumes of *Miscanthus sinensis* complement the clusters of orange-red fruits on *Idesia polycarpa*.

Winter is also the time to make the most of the beauty of certain conifers and the delicacy of many grasses. Springing from a carpet of mauve heathers and surrounded by two *Abies procera* 'Glauca', *Pinus sylvestris* 'Gold Medal' awaits the cold weather which will transform it into a sunny colour. *Saccharum ravennae* and the *Miscanthus sinensis* cultivars 'Cosmopolitan' and 'Morning Light' powdered with snow add a touch of lightness to the composition.

THE SIR HAROLD HILLIER GARDENS

Sir Harold Hillier, a renowned nurseryman, had a great influence on contemporary horticulture. Starting in 1953, he began to plant many rare trees on the banks of the River Test, about six miles north-west of Southampton. This arboretum became one of the richest and most beautiful collections of temperate-climate woody plants in the world. The figures are dizzying: no less than 14 national collections, 42,000 trees and shrubs, 12,000 different taxa, all on a 178 acre landscaped site. It is a paradise on earth for plant lovers.

The diversity of the very popular winter garden, created in 1996, is also impressive. It has been extended three times in order to display the plants to their best advantage. With almost 650 different species in an area covering 4 acres, it offers hundreds of plant combinations. Indeed, in the Hillier Gardens winter is always an attractive season. The luminous colours and amazing textures of the bark of *Betula*, *Prunus*, *Acer*, *Stewartia*, *Cornus*, *Rubus* and *Salix* easily hold their own alongside the intoxicating blooms of *Daphne*, *Hamamelis*, *Lonicera*, *Viburnum*, *Galanthus* and *Cyclamen*.

The eastern end of the garden contains an incredible collection of dwarf conifers adjoining the collection of heathers planted in the 1960s. These plantings are constantly evolving, replanted every ten years with recent cultivars. They provide many ideas about complementary planting for the winter garden and offer striking forms and colours that contrast with the white trunks of Himalayan birches.

Set among *Carex morrowii* 'Fisher's Form', scarlet *Cornus alba* 'Sibirica' lights up in the low winter sun.

TOP: *Cornus sanguinea* 'Midwinter Fire' takes up a lot of room when in full leaf.
ABOVE: One has to wait until winter to enjoy its main attraction: colourful wood that gives warmth to the garden while at the same time adding a feeling of transparency to the planting. The trunks of *Betula ermanii* and its cultivar 'Grayswood Hill' are wonderfully enhanced.

TOP: The yellow leaves of *Hamamelis × intermedia* 'Savill Starlight' accompany
the handsome pinkish-red autumnal appearance of *Cornus alba* 'Sibirica'.
ABOVE: Once the dogwoods are bare of leaves, the striking black silhouette of
Pittosporum tenuifolium 'Tom Thumb' can be seen. In the background *Betula
albosinensis* 'Bowling Green' reveals its lovely bark.

Consider using gentle pastel shades, just as effective as more vivid plants. The white *Betula utilis* form the structure of this scene. The acid-yellow flowers of *Hamamelis × intermedia* 'Savill Starlight' and *Helleborus × hybridus* marry harmoniously with the lime-green stems of *Cornus sericea* 'Flaviramea'. The blue of *Picea glauca* 'Alberta Blue' combines perfectly with the mauve of *Erica carnea* 'Pink Mist', delicately setting off the dominant colour of this planting.

TOP: The red stems of *Cornus alba* 'Sibirica' stand out among the orange-yellow culms of
Phyllostachys aureosulcata f. *spectabilis*. ABOVE: Black *Ophiopogon planiscapus* 'Nigrescens'
contrasts with the golden foliage and white branches of *Rubus cockburnianus* 'Goldenvale'.
RIGHT: The severity of balls of box and the long leaves of *Dianella tasmanica* 'Emerald
Arch' juxtapose with the light, twisted shape of *Salix* × 'Erythroflexuosa'.

LEFT: Beneath trees, bulbs make an excellent ephemeral groundcover, as seen here with *Cyclamen coum* and *Galanthus nivalis* under a majestic *Carpinus betulus* 'Fastigiata'. ABOVE: Rarely used in winter gardens, *Stewartia pseudocamellia* is nevertheless a delight with its graceful habit and the orange-grey bark it acquires as it ages. It also flowers magnificently in early summer and turns flaming orange-red in autumn.

Conifers and heathers act as links and give structure to the garden. Their very varied textures and habits add colour and rhythm. Among those with golden foliage are *Chamaecyparis obtusa* 'Spiralis Aurea' and *Chamaecyparis obtusa* 'Nana Aurea' (TOP) and *Pinus sylvestris* 'Gold Medal', a must, with the heather *Erica arborea* 'Albert's Gold' (ABOVE) beneath it.

RIGHT: Thanks to its variegated leaves which catch the light, *Juniperus chinensis* 'Japonica Variegata' seems to be lit from within.

Two *Acer griseum* stand guard as colours change with the approach of winter. Beneath them the bed of *Euonymus fortunei* 'Emerald 'n' Gold' turns from yellow to a pinkish orange. In the centre the imposing planting of *Rubus cockburnianus* 'Goldenvale' turns from golden to pinkish-white. *Pinus mugo* 'Winter Gold', in a row in the background, becomes gold in winter while beneath them *Mahonia aquifolium* 'Apollo' takes on a purple-black hue.

BRESSINGHAM GARDENS

Situated some 50 miles north-east of Cambridge, Bressingham Gardens are the creation of the Bloom family, nurserymen who have had a considerable influence on horticulture for decades. On this 15-acre site more than 8,000 species are displayed in six beautiful themed gardens.

Alan Bloom was known worldwide for his unique collection of perennials. In 1962, his son Adrian joined the family business and began to diversify the nursery's range of plants with heathers and dwarf and low-growing conifers. He then began his first, very successful, experiments with planting for winter.

In 1967, he set out to create a garden that would be attractive throughout the year – Foggy Bottom, probably the first landscape design conceived as a winter garden. On almost 6 acres, more than 500 different conifers contrasted with a hundred or so heathers and a few plants grown for their bark. Over the course of the years the garden has continued to evolve. The heathers disappeared to make room for the now mature conifers, for a collection of trees and shrubs, for ornamental grasses and for many perennials.

In 2003 Adrian designed a new garden devoted exclusively to winter. The site chosen was near the main entrance in order to make this garden accessible to the greatest number of visitors. In a small ½ acre area it contains about 250 species whose winter flowers or fruits, scents, barks and different colours of evergreen foliage blend harmoniously. The spectacular repeat plantings of dogwoods, birches, conifers, heathers, bergenias and grasses are emblematic of this majestic composition.

In winter the purple river of *Bergenia* 'Bressingham Ruby' flows between the orange-tinted leaves of *Libertia peregrinans* 'Gold Leaf' and the flaming stems of *Cornus sanguinea* 'Midwinter Fire'.

Ordinary-looking when in leaf, *Cornus sanguinea* 'Midwinter Fire' rapidly becomes a winter attraction with its bright orange stems. Beneath it the silvery-blue tufts of *Festuca glauca* 'Elijah Blue' marry prettily with the mauve of *Erica carnea* 'Pink Spangles', while *Pinus mugo* 'Carsten', a dwarf conifer, takes on handsome golden tints with the first frosts.

In the middle of winter warm tones awaken the garden. At this time of year
Abies nordmanniana 'Golden Spreader', in the foreground, becomes amber-yellow.
The imposing massed *Cornus sanguinea* 'Midwinter Fire', truly blazing, provide
a solid block of colour ideal for setting off the three small *Betula apoiensis*
'Mount Apoi' and the blue-green ball of *Pinus pumila* 'Globe'.

TOP: The parallel rows of *Cornus* 'Midwinter Fire' and balls of the blueish *Picea sitchensis* 'Tenas' as well as of the greener *Pinus heldreichii* 'Smidtii' give this scene a masterly rhythm.

ABOVE AND RIGHT: The trio of *Chionochloa rubra*, *Bergenia* 'Bressingham Ruby' and *Cornus* 'Sibirica' is repeated several times in this dynamic composition. *Helleborus* × *nigercors* is planted here and there and the picture is completed with the white trunks of *Betula utilis* var. *jacquemontii* 'Grayswood Ghost' standing out against a background of blue-grey *Cupressus* 'Blue Ice'.

This design for winter has been conceived of as a painting. The artist-gardener
has a large plant palette from which to add touches of colour. He makes use of
the coloured stems of dogwoods and willows, the branches of birch trees, the
colourful evergreen foliage of dwarf conifers, carpets of heathers and grasses as
well as the dark dry flower heads of sedums.

TOP, AND RIGHT: Conifers offer unusual growth habits and very varied colours. An arching
Cedrus atlantica 'Glauca Pendula' and the graceful light green sentinels of *Xanthocyparis*
nootkatensis 'Green Arrow' give structure to this garden.

ABOVE: Other plants take on a new colour in winter: coppery for *Microbiota decussata* in
the right-hand corner, golden for *Abies nordmanniana* 'Golden Spreader' and *Pinus mugo*
'Carsten' just above it, and bronze for the two *Thuja occidentalis* 'Barabit's Gold' on the left.

ABOVE: In the lower part of Foggy Bottom, the many conifers remind us of the early days of this garden and its importance in the history of modern winter gardens.
LEFT: This unique collection of conifers provides a wonderful setting for the red-stemmed *Acer* × *conspicuum* 'Phoenix' and for *Betula papyrifera* with their white trunks and orange autumn leaves.

Even without plants grown for their bark it is possible to create an attractive design for
winter using only the colours of evergreen foliage and a diversity of forms and textures.
Grasses (*Stipa tenuissima*, *Festuca* 'Blaufuchs' and *Festuca gautieri*) add lightness and a
contemporary feel which goes perfectly with the mysterious *Cedrus atlantica* 'Glauca
Pendula'. At ground level the handsome purple leaves of *Heuchera* 'Prince' fill in the gaps.

WINTER GARDENS

SOURCES
OF INSPIRATION

HARLOW CARR

The youngest of the Royal Horticultural Society's four flagship gardens is situated about 20 miles north of Leeds. Its Winter Walk, covering an area of more than 2,000 square metres, was created in 2006 to brighten the garden during the dark days of winter and thus to attract more visitors. At the beginning, priority was given to plants with brightly coloured stems. Then trees with ornamental bark, colourful foliage, flowering and scented shrubs, structural evergreens, decorative perennials and thousands of bulbs were added to create a harmonious and magical scene. This incredible richness offers a stunning spectacle, constantly renewed from mid-autumn to early spring.

The many colours and different heights of *Rubus thibetanus* 'Silver Fern',
Salix 'Britzensis', and the *Cornus* cultivars 'Sibirica', 'Kesselringii' and
'Midwinter Fire' give rhythm to this planting. The flowers of *Sarcococca
hookeriana* var. *digyna* and *Viburnum* × *bodnantense* 'Charles Lamont'
perfume the air. The striking trunks of *Betula albosinensis* 'Fascination' and
the tall *Fagus sylvatica* 'Pendula' serve as punctuation marks.

Winter heathers make excellent groundcovers, adding important colour
to plantings. The numerous cultivars of *Erica carnea* and *Erica × darleyensis*
among others provide a range of colours from white to orange shades,
via pink, mauve, red and purple. These heathers are most effective when
associated with dwarf conifers or plants with coloured stems.

Once you have chosen a good combination of plants, you can repeat it over a larger area.
TOP: The variegated leaves of *Yucca filamentosa* 'Bright Edge' and *Helleborus × hybridus*
'Harvington Yellow Speckled' make a good transition between the bright red *Cornus alba*
'Sibirica' and the orange-yellow *Cornus sanguinea* 'Midwinter Fire'.
ABOVE: The red stems of *Cornus alba* 'Aurea' contrast even better with *Betula utilis* var.
jacquemontii than the yellow stems of *Cornus sericea* 'Flaviramea'.

Playing with the form, texture and colour of different plant parts (leaves/flowers/ stems) is the best way to bring out the decorative elements of a particular plant. TOP: The fine branches of *Cornus sanguinea* 'Midwinter Fire' emerge from the large round leaves of *Bergenia* 'Overture'. ABOVE: The graceful acid-green tufts of *Carex oshimensis* 'Evergold' planted en masse show off the mahogany-coloured stems of *Cornus alba* 'Kesselringii'.

JARDINS DE BELLEVUE

Half-way between Rouen and Dieppe, hellebores hold sway. The whole family of gardeners here is passionate about this amazing plant which, heedless of the cold, bravely and generously opens wide its petals. Martine Lemonnier, the owner of this garden, has specialized in hybridizing this plant and has formed one of the richest collections of hellebores in Europe – indeed, she holds the French national collections of hellebores and of the blue Himalayan poppy. Created in 1980, this magnificent 15-acre garden contains many other treasures, including many of the plants with striking bark that light up gardens at all times of year.

LEFT: *Prunus rufa* (the lighter-coloured Cambridge clone) stands out in front of the powerfully scented *Sarcococca confusa*. Beneath it are the greenish flowers of *Ribes laurifolium* and a carpet of *Helleborus × lemonnierae*. The final touch is provided by the discreet and delicately scented pink blossom of *Prunus mume* 'Beni Chidori'.
ABOVE: The only hellebore that Martine Lemmonier allows to naturalize beneath the birches is *Helleborus argutifolius* with its luminous acid-green flowers.

About 40 miles north-east of London, Marks Hall Gardens & Arboretum cover almost 200 acres. Here visitors can admire the 18th-century walled garden, the forest of Wollemi Pines, the thousands of snowdrops growing beneath the trees and the winter garden. The Birkett Long Millennium Walk, created in 2000 and about 200m long, forms a living picture renewed continuously from autumn to early spring. Repeated mass planting of a few emblematic species from Asia is highly effective, giving a sense of purity and harmony. The reflections of the plants in the lake make the scene even more spectacular.

There was no need to use many different plant varieties to make this garden a paradise. Skilfully deployed, *Betula utilis* var. *jacquemontii*, *Cornus alba* 'Sibirica', *Miscanthus* 'Kleine Fontaine', *Rubus thibetanus* and *Sarcococca hookeriana* var. *digyna* are the five key plants repeated again and again all along the Millennium Walk.

TOP, AND RIGHT: When beauty and simplicity meet…
Once its leaves have fallen, in autumn *Cornus alba* 'Sibirica'
glows in front of the monotone hues of natural woodland.
ABOVE: The generous yellow flowers of *Hamamelis mollis*
give off a subtle scent for a long period in winter.

LA POMMERAIE

Patrick Garçonnet's garden, La Pommeraie, situated about 6 miles south-east of Dieppe and covering an area of 5,000 square metres, contains an unforgettable collection of trees with ornamental bark. On one of his visits to the Hennebelle nursery in 1989, the purity of the Himalayan white birch opened Patrick's eyes to the beauty of bark. He realized that birches, cinnamon and snakebark maples, cherries and indeed dogwoods and willows with coloured stems would become the key features of his plantings. He created among other things a replica of Jean-Pierre Hennebelle's famous bark grove, a planting that has now become emblematic of La Pommeraie. It includes several white or pastel-coloured varieties of birch (*Betula utilis* var. *jacquemontii*, *Betula albosinensis* var. *septentrionalis*, *Betula nigra* 'Heritage') which contrast with the more brightly-coloured bark of *Prunus serrula*, *Acer griseum* and *Cornus alba* 'Westonbirt'.

TOP: In autumn the stems of dogwoods go perfectly with the trunks of birches, maples and cherries. This plant association remains attractive all winter long. ABOVE: With a *Betula costata* on its left and a *Betula albosinensis* on its right, *Cornus alba* 'Westonbirt' is the first to lose its leaves and display the luminous red stems that rapidly light up the garden.

LADY FARM GARDENS

Lost in the middle of the countryside, surrounded by the dairy cows and arable land of
the Chew Valley, Lady Farm Gardens are situated about 7 miles south of Bristol. Judy
Pearce, their owner and creator, was determined to design a garden that would combine
minimum maintenance with maximum ornamental interest throughout the year. The
gardens are now known for the magnificent informal wild spaces, such as the Prairie and
the Steppe, created in 1997. Grasses rule at Lady Farm, an unforgettable sight when their
feathery plumes are touched by hoar frost or catch the rays of the sun.

Winter is coming, bringing the first frosts. As it rises, the sun touches
the imposing plumes of *Cortaderia* 'Sunningdale Silver' and the delicate
inflorescences of *Stipa gigantea*. A little later it will be the turn of the
two specimens of *Cortaderia richardii* in the second rank and of the
Miscanthus transmorrisonensis on the left to light up. The red stems of
Cornus alba 'Westonbirt' then make the planting blaze.

RIGHT: Hoar frost adds a touch of magic, instantly bringing out the decorativeness of even the most ordinary plants. The old oak is impressive in the white landscape.
ABOVE: Every detail is finely picked out, showing off the blackened flower heads of *Phlomis russeliana* and the variegated leaves of the grasses (*Miscanthus sinensis* 'Gracillimus' and 'Ferner Osten', *Deschampsia cespitosa* 'Goldtau').

Created more than 25 years go by the landscape designer and writer Kathy Brown, The Manor House is about 40 miles west of Cambridge. Its four-season gardens, covering almost 5 acres, consist of twenty or so different scenes, each with its own particular atmosphere. The owner draws her inspiration from works by the artists she loves, such as Hepworth, Monet, Kandinsky, Hokusai, Rothko and Mondrian. Set off by even the slightest ray of sunlight, grasses play a major role in all her plantings, especially in the birch avenue created in 1998 which has become one of the emblems of the garden.

The combination of grasses and birches is always effective. The blueish
tufts of *Helictotrichon sempervirens* and *Festuca glauca* form a homogenous
framework with the mother-of-pearl plumes of *Cortaderia selloana* 'Pumila'
and the erect stems of *Calamagrostis* × *acutiflora* 'Overdam'. Against
this canvas of grasses, the ghostly trunks of *Betula utilis* var. *jacquemontii*
'Grayswood Ghost' stand out with gentle elegance.

CAMBRIDGE UNIVERSITY BOTANIC GARDEN

More than one and a half centuries old, this botanic garden played a vital role in the emergence and development of the winter garden. In 1951, on an area of barely 1 acre, a few species that were expected to look good in winter were planted in a strictly academic manner so that they could be studied. From 1978 onwards this experimental arrangement has been completely transformed into a landscaped winter garden and has become a model example. The evergreen hedges that surround it give it an intimate atmosphere, providing a dark, homogenous background which sets off the plants perfectly. They also help to channel the scents of the winter-flowering plants concentrated on both sides of the central path that winds between the colourful beds.

The upright red branches of *Cornus alba* 'Sibirica' make an
elegant contrast with the lime-green flowers of *Helleborus
foetidus* and the white-variegated foliage of *Euonymus fortunei*
'Silver Queen'. Avoid spindle-trees with too much yellow
variegation as they often look too aggressive.

ABOVE: Still bearing its autumn leaves, *Cornus alba* 'Sibirica' stands out, framed by green foliage. During the winter this foliage will change colour to harmonize with the red dogwoods. *Bergenia* 'Bressingham Ruby' has now taken on a purple hue, *Erica* 'Furzey' is opening its pale mauve buds and the palmate leaves of *Helleborus foetidus* have become a darker green. RIGHT: Seen against the light, the peeling bark of *Acer griseum* glows, as do the stems of *Rubus phoenicolasius* and *Cornus sanguinea* 'Midwinter Fire'.

WISLEY

This temple of botany is the crown jewel of the Royal Horticultural Society's gardens. Its 240 acres, situated on the south-western outskirts of Greater London, contain one of the finest collections of plants in the world. At Wisley, winter as a season was reinvented decades ago. The national collection of heathers, the pinetum, the monumental glasshouse for exotics and the incredible diversity of plants with ornamental bark are well worth seeing. The main winter planting is around the ponds in Seven Acres. The Winter Walk, begun in 2002 and completed in 2013, is dominated by the multicoloured stems of dogwoods, willows, brambles and maples.

LEFT: The undulating white stems of *Rubus cockburnianus* 'Goldenvale' make a bold and colourful combination with *Cornus* 'Budd's Yellow' against a red background of *Cornus alba* 'Sibirica'. TOP: Pollarded *Acer negundo* 'Winter Lightning' shows off its luminous acid-yellow young branches in front of glowing *Cornus* 'Anny's Winter Orange'. ABOVE: The orange branches of *Salix alba* 'Yelverton' interweave with the white stems of *Rubus cockburnianus*.

For several months, the *Cornus* and *Rubus* used here form a massed
linear planting of about the same height, with leaves that blend
together without any real demarcation. There is always a risk that,
if the trees are all deciduous, once their leaves have fallen the scene
risks becoming less eye-catching and losing its intensity.

In this example, the planting can be read at more and better defined levels: *Rubus cockburnianus* 'Goldenvale' adds rhythm with its almost rampant habit and weaves its way into the upright red stems of *Cornus alba* 'Sibirica'. The small contrasting touch given by mostly dark evergreen foliage in the second rank provides better structure to the planting and improves its readability.

ABOVE: Don't be afraid of using unusual forms of trees in your plantings: in the foreground the mysterious weeping shape of *Cedrus atlantica* 'Glauca Pendula' and in the background the bottle-shaped trunk and spreading habit of the imposing *Metasequoia glyptostroboides* (top) or *Araucaria araucana* with its branches in regular tiers (bottom).

RIGHT: With its feet among pink heathers and its head in the conifers, *Betula ermanii* × *pubescens* shows off its white skin.

Alex, Nathalie and Flore Bachelet are true plantspeople. They love unusual, curious and striking plants, which they bring back from their botanic trips to Holland, Germany and Great Britain. In 1995, they gathered their finds together at Le Clos du Verbosc, a garden covering 5 acres siuated in the Yvetot region, around 19 miles north-west of Rouen. Their collections of Japanese maples, dogwoods, magnolias and above all of every kind of plant with ornamental bark combine harmoniously to create an unforgettable sight in all seasons.

ABOVE: The cinnamon colour of the flower heads of *Hydrangea paniculata* 'Grandiflora' repeats the colour of the bark of *Betula albosinensis* 'Princesse Sturdza' on their left and of the two *Acer griseum* on either side.

LEFT: The *Heuchera* cultivars 'Obsidian' and 'Caramel' form a simple and elegant carpet beneath the light-coloured trunks of *Betula*.

STONE LANE GARDENS

Stone Lane lies some 30 miles north-east of Plymouth, on the edge of the Dartmoor National Park. Its creator, Kenneth Ashburner, began planting in 1971 using only seeds collected from the wild. Today the 5-acre arboretum is home to the national collections of alders and birches, the latter being one of the richest collections in England with around 70 different taxa. It is without doubt the best place to admire the incredible richness of barks in this genus, taking you on a journey through the birch forests of the world, from Canada and the United States through Europe to the Himalayas and Japan.

LEFT: *Betula ermanii* 'Grayswood Hill', like all the cultivars of this species, takes on magnificent autumn colour. TOP: The trunks of *Betula ermanii* 'Grayswood Hill', usually creamy white, combine perfectly with the more orange tones of *Betula albosinensis* var. *septentrionalis* on the right. ABOVE: If you enjoy contrasts, give pride of place to *Betula utilis* 'Mount Luoji' whose trunks have shades ranging from coppery red to deep purple.

All the trees in this birch wood were grown from seed collected in the wild.
Betula ermanii develops pale trunks in many shades of cream. Although from
the same origin, the small grove of *Betula albosinensis* shows a subtle genetic
variation, to the delight of gardeners. This has led to two cultivars: 'China
Rose' with a deeper colour tending to orange-red, and 'Pink Champagne' with
pale pink tones.

LE PERDRIER

Just outside Nantes, on the banks of the River Erdre, Jean-Charles Chiron designed Le Perdrier in a style both contemporary and refined. Inspired by the simplicity of Japanese gardens, this landscape architect put his ideas into practice and continues all the time to experiment with new concepts. The 6,000 square metre garden is based on a few fine collectors' plants with a focus on autumn foliage and bark. His favourite tree is the mahogany-skinned *Prunus serrula* which he sets off with a bright red wall containing a circular hole, a protective symbol in Japan. A judicious choice of plants, regular plant forms and the many walls give this garden its perfect structure, while its gentleness and refinement carry you off to the Land of the Rising Sun.

LEFT AND TOP: Walls serve to open up perspectives, help us to
discover the garden slowly, and act as a screen against which
the architectural shadows of bare branches are projected.
ABOVE: Slate monoliths make an ideal foreground for the stems
of the giant Kamchatka horsetail (*Equisetum camtschatcense*).

Le Vasterival is situated on the Albâtre coast, about 6 miles west of Dieppe. Covering about 30 acres, this jewel among French gardens is home to thousands of botanical treasures. Le Vasterival was created in the 1950s by Princess Greta Sturdza and rapidly became a model for its judicious selection of plants and the harmonious combinations that make the garden beautiful all year round. From early on, Princess Sturdza chose plants that were of ornamental interest in winter. She focused in particular on decorative bark as well as on winter-flowering species, for example hellebores, skimmias and witch hazels.

In the maple grove at the bottom of the garden, trees with ornamental
bark follow one after another to make a handsome line: reddish *Prunus
maacki*, darker *Prunus serrula × serrulata* and white *Betula utilis* var.
jacquemontii, with a large *Cornus officinalis* showing off its dazzling early
yellow flowers and white patches of flowering *Galanthus*.

TOP: The orange flowers of *Hamamelis*, the mauve cushions of *Calluna*, the pastel-coloured trunks of *Betula nigra* and *Betula albosinsensis*, the golden stems of *Salix babylonica* and the blueish branches of *Acer tegmentosum*… winter is definitely a colourful season!

ABOVE: Attention to detail often leads to an attractive fusion: the rusty-coloured down on the underside of the leaves of *Rhododendron yakushimanum* × *bureavii* goes beautifully with the orange stems of *Cornus* 'Winter Flame'.

The rosy-red buds of *Skimmia anquetilia* in the foreground
with the cultivar *Skimmia japonica* 'Rubella' behind them go
perfectly with the fiery young shoots of *Acer palmatum*
'Eddisbury'. The yellow flowers of *Hamamelis × intermedia*
'Arnold Promise' add a touch of freshness to the composition.

ROSEMOOR

Situated about 50 miles north of Plymouth in the Torridge valley, this famous garden of the Royal Horticultural Society is one of the most beautiful horticultural jewels in South-West England. Nestling among woodland, Rosemoor's 65 acres offer wonderful plant combinations where textures, colours and scents mingle in succession over the course of the seasons. Created in 1996, the winter garden has now reached maturity. Its coloured stems and ornamental barks are accompanied by exuberant winter flowers and striking evergreens that give structure to the garden. The Foliage Garden also offers an amazing multicoloured spectacle and enriches the plant palette available in this season.

The light green columns of *Thuja occidentalis* 'Smaragd', the orange tuft of *Hakonechloa macra* and the straw-coloured culms of *Panicum virgatum* 'Shenandoah' set off the greyish-white trunk of the *Eucalyptus pauciflora* subsp. *niphophila* that dominates the Foliage Garden.

TOP: The impressive *Mahonia × media* 'Buckland' forms an ideal backdrop to *Cornus alba* 'Sibirica', while its golden flowering spikes echo the variegated foliage of *Euonymus fortunei* 'Emerald 'n' Gold' in the foreground.
ABOVE: The orange-yellow canes of *Phyllostachys aureosulcata* f. *spectabilis* rise from a bed of *Stipa*, *Miscanthus*, *Molinia* and other grasses.

Ever since its creation in the 1930s, The Savill Garden has been a source of inspiration for generations of plant lovers. It covers 35 acres in the eastern part of the Royal Park of Windsor. Every season here is a festival of colours and scents. Once autumn ends, the bright flowers of the collections of mahonias and witch hazels light up the garden. Grasses, euphorbias and New Zealand species give structure and striking textures. What is more, since 2008 a show has been guaranteed by a spectacular winter garden which gives prime place to ornamental bark and coloured stems. in particular those of dogwoods and willows planted en masse.

The pale green and acid-yellow of various leaves and flowers (*Skimmia japonica* 'Winifred Crook', *Helleborus argutifolius*, *Hamamelis × intermedia* 'Pallida', *Platycladus orientalis* 'Pyramidalis Aurea') interspersed with different touches of red create a fine symphony of colour. The arching stems of *Rubus phoenicolasius* echo the red bark of *Acer × conspicuum* 'Phoenix' and *Prunus rufa*. In the background *Cornus* 'Anny's Winter Orange' completes this colourful scene.

TOP: When they are planted as specimen trees, it is better to coppice *Betula utilis* var. *jacquemontii* 'Grayswood Ghost'. The multiple trunks have a natural beauty, set off by the golden stems of *Salix alba* 'Golden Ness'.
ABOVE: In other situations, the stiffness of the single trunks of *Betula utilis* 'Doorenbos' goes better with the flaring habit of *Cornus alba* 'Sibirica', *Cornus sanguinea* 'Midwinter Fire' and *Cornus sericea* 'Flaviramea'

TOP: In the left foreground *Salix alba* 'Yelverton' glows with a slightly more intense orange than its counterpart *Salix alba* 'Britzensis' on the right.
ABOVE: The ghostly stems of *Acer tegmentosum* 'Valley Phantom' are worthy of the cultivar name. They rise from a carpet that becomes darker in winter: *Microbiota decussata* takes on a bronze tint while *Bergenia* 'Overture' becomes purplish, against a background of different-coloured *Cornus*.

LA MARE AUX TREMBLES

Near a pool once bordered with aspens (in French *trembles*), the intimate garden created by Thérèse and Pierre Gibert in 1995 extends over 11 acres. It is situated in a small Normandy village about 20 miles south-west of Rouen. Winter seemed sad and dreary in their peaceful haven, so after reading *La Bruyère*, Monsieur de La Rochefoucauld's monograph on heathers, and visiting his arboretum Les Grandes Bruyères, the couple began to use heathers to give their garden the final touch that it lacked.

This floriferous groundcover is used extensively along the central path, alongside witch hazels and trees with ornamental bark. The ten white Himalayan birches planted on a moss lawn contrast with the rest of the garden. The play of reflections in the ornamental pond, small though it is, is an essential element in this minimalist composition.

TOP: Evergreen topiary (balls, billows) are fitted in like a "crazy patchwork", another activity about which Thérèse is passionate. ABOVE: Set among heathers, the white trunk of *Betula utilis* var. *jacquemontii* enables the coppery bark of *Acer griseum* and the red flowers of *Hamamelis* × *intermedia* 'Diane' to look good without clashing.

ANGLESEY ABBEY

Situated some 6 miles north-east of Cambridge, Anglesey Abbey has made winter one of its best seasons. Thousands of snowdrops whiten the ground beneath the trees. Using a palette of more than 200 plants, the winter garden created in 1996 winds along for nearly ¼ of a mile. Scenes succeed one another, with an emphasis on mass effects and repeated plantings of scented plants and those with coloured stems, bark and foliage. The narrow path ends with a unique planting of almost 120 white Himalayan birches, whose pristine trunks contrast well with the dark colour of the mulch on the bare soil.

The blueish foliage finely outlined in creamy white of *Euphorbia characias* 'White Swan' is the detail which makes this pairing with *Cornus alba* 'Westonbirt' so successful.

The effect of a limited selection of species planted en masse is spectacular. TOP: The holly-like leaves of *Mahonia aquifolium* 'Apollo' take on a purple-black hue in winter. Its dense mass sets off the orange-yellow stems of *Salix alba* var. *vitellina* and its cultivar 'Britzensis'. BOTTOM: In the same way, *Cornus sanguinea* 'Winter Beauty' creates an orange mass from which the multiple trunks of *Prunus serrula* stand out.

ABOVE: Have the courage to go for plant associations that offer strong contrasts: the acid yellow-green leaves of *Luzula sylvatica* 'Aurea' set against a background of dark purple *Mahonia aquifolium* 'Apollo'; the orange stems of *Cornus sanguinea* 'Winter Beauty' and the golden-yellow flowers of *Hamamelis × intermedia* 'Pallida' rise from a black carpet of *Ophiopogon planiscapus* 'Nigrescens'.

Combinations of plants whose colours are soft and harmonious
are just as effective. The white margins of the light green leaves
of *Euonymus fortunei* 'Emerald Gaiety' tend to turn pink in winter.
This spindle-tree goes beautifully with the sweetly scented *Viburnum
× bodnantense* 'Dawn' growing above it. The flowers of *Hamamelis ×
intermedia* 'Barmstedt Gold' add a sunny touch to the scene.

The Winter Walk ends in a striking planting, very contemporary in style, of more than a hundred *Betula utilis* var. *jacquemontii*. In order to maintain their immaculate whiteness, the trunks of these trees are carefully cleaned with a high-pressure hose every year at the end of November. In spring, 4,000 bulbs of *Tulipa* 'Little Beauty' cover the ground in dark red, changing the scene dramatically.

WINTER GARDENS
THE PLANT PALETTE

(JARDIN DU BOIS MARQUIS - FRANCE)

DECORATIVE BARK

Bark is a decorative element offering a whole range of bright and lumincus colours. It is the key feature of winter gardens. However, an understanding of what gives bark its colour is essential if we are to make good use of it. Here are some of the mainstay plants with ornamental bark, as well as others that are less widely used but just as spectacular.

GENETICS

The characteristics of a plant chosen for its ornamental bark are deeply connected to its genes. Genetic selection always leads to pleasant surprises, giving nuances of colour much sought after by gardeners.

(STONE LANE GARDENS, ENGLAND)

LEFT: In this little birch grove, the mauve and salmon-pink trunks all belong to natural hybrids of *Betula albosinensis*. All the seeds were collected in the wild at Kaolan, in the Gansu province of North-West China. In spite of their common origin there is a marked genetic variability, with some seeds giving rise to trees with more strongly coloured bark. This has led to the creation of two cultivars: 'China Rose' whose bark is a brighter pink, veering towards an orange-red, and 'Pink Champagne' with paler pink bark.

BELOW: It is important to choose a good clone which will show the desired colour. For example, Hillier's clone of *Prunus rufa* is darker than the Cambridge clone. *Acer griseum* can be propagated only from seed. Depending on the origin of the mother plants bearing fertile seeds, the trunks of this maple show variations in peeling as well as colours ranging from ochre (1a) to red (1b) to almost black (1c).

[1a]

[1b]

[1c]

ENVIRONMENT

It is not the genotype alone that is responsible for the phenotype. Growing conditions also have a considerable influence on bark colour. Climate, humidity, exposure and soil type also need to be taken into consideration.

(MOUNT FIELD NATIONAL PARK, TASMANIA, AUSTRALIA)

ABOVE: To witness the rainbow-coloured bark of this *Eucalyptus coccifera*, it is essential to bring together all the favourable environmental factors. The particular soil of the high plateaux of Tasmania, the altitude, the cool temperatures, the presence of fog saturating the atmosphere with moisture, not to mention the peeling period that reveals the colour variations on the trunks – it is hard to achieve an adequate combination of all these factors in order to be able to admire this spectacular but alas transitory spectacle.

RIGHT: This birch (2a) is the mother plant that provided grafting material for all the *Betula albosinensis* Blason® 'Minrouge'. It grows in the Jardin du Bois Marquis at Vernioz, south of Lyon, while one of its first clones (2b) flourishes in the garden of L'Étang de Launay at Varengeville-sur-Mer near Dieppe. The climate, humidity, exposure and soil are so different here that the second birch shows a much more brightly coloured bark than the specimen from which it was propagated.

[2a]

[2b]

AGE

Betula, *Prunus* and *Acer* all show attractive and well-marked bark from an early age. Some trunks require patience, however, if you are to admire their beautifully coloured patches.

[4]

(PARC DE LA TÊTE D'OR, FRANCE)

[5]

(GIARDINI BOTANICI DI VILLA TARANTO, ITALY)

[1a]

[1b]

[2a]

[6]

(ARNOLD ARBORETUM, USA)

Trees are subject to great tensions as their diameters expand. Bark that is at first fine and smooth progressively develops cracks, discolorations and fissures, becomes corky or peels. In a young *Melia azedarach* (1a) the satiny and sometimes reddish bark is covered in lenticels. A few decades later deep grooves have formed (1b).

It is easy to see the process of increasing corkiness on a specimen of *Acer palmatum* 'Arakawa': the young green bark (2a) is slowly covered in a crust of scaly cork, giving the old trunk a strikingly reptilian appearance (2b). As the tree ages, the salmon-pink colour (3a) of a young *Betula nigra* darkens, hence the name black birch (3b). *Pinus bungeana* [4] is not often planted because of its very slow growth rate. One has to wait many years to enjoy its most handsome characteristic. Its bark then starts to resemble that of a plane tree before becoming white in old specimens. In the same way, the orange scales of *Stewartia pseudocamellia* [5] or *Zelkova sinica* [6] don't start spreading on the trunks and branches until the tree has reached a fairly advanced age.

[3b]

[5a]

[5b]

THE SHEDDING PERIOD

Changes in the colour of bark occur principally when the trees shed their skin annually in the form of patches or strips.

This transitional period always offers an amazing range of colours. As it falls, the old bark contrasts with the freshly exposed new bark. Depending on the species, this phenomenon can last from a few days to several weeks. It may also start at different times of year: in late spring for various *Arbutus* species, in full summer for the much-loved *Platanus* × *acerifolia* and many *Eucalyptus* species, and in autumn for *Stewartia pseudocamellia*.

ABOVE: In winter *Stewartia sinensis* changes its skin: from a majestic mauve it beomes yellowish before finally turning greenish grey.

RIGHT: The bark of *Betula gynoterminalis* gets darker as it ages, taking on a wine-red or dark purple hue (1a). As the old bark peels it splits to reveal an olive green colour (1b).

[1a]

[1b]

SEASONS

A few plants don't need to shed their leaves to change their appearance when the cold starts to bite and the sap stops rising. Winter works its magic subtly.

ABOVE: Usually a shade of orange, the bark of *Acer conspicuum* × 'Phoenix' begins to turn pink in autumn before becoming scarlet in mid-winter.

BELOW: Similar changes in the colour of their bark are seen in other snakebark maples: *Acer pensylvanicum* 'Erythrocladum' changes from yellow (2a) to a more pronounced orange (2b), while the green bark of *Acer pectinatum* 'Sirene' is transformed into a startling carmine. In winter the vigorous bright green branches of *Acer negundo* 'Winter Lightning' (3a) light up into an amazingly luminous yellow (3b). These changes in pigmentation in winter are also frequent in many *Cornus* varieties with coloured wood.

[2a] [2b] [3a] [3b]

EXPOSURE AND HUMIDITY

Exposure to sun and humidity, either momentary due to a storm or lasting due to significant annual rainfall, inevitably has an effect on the colours of bark.

[5a]

[5b]

(JARDIN DU BOIS MARQUIS, FRANCE)

[1a]

[1b]

[2]

In the shade behind an imposing yew hedge, *Betula* 'Hergest' displays markedly orange bark (1a). A clone growing only a few yards away but this time in front of the hedge, giving it a very different exposure, is entirely white (1b).

Without anything in front of it to filter the direct sunlight, the delicate bark of this *Acer davidii* 'Viper' has become brown on the side exposed to the full sun [2]. By contrast, on its north-facing side the marbled bark retains its characteristic green and white veining. After rain or morning dew, moisture intensifies the colours of bark. The orange-brown trunk (5a) of *Arbutus × andrachnoides* (Jardin du Bois Marquis) becomes bright orange-red when wet (5b).

Sometimes water can even make colours appear that are invisible to the naked eye when the bark is dry. This curious phenomenon is easily seen in *Platanus × acerifolia*: after a summer storm the patches of bark that were greyish (4a) turn green as if by magic, while the yellow patches become more intense (4b). A high degree of moisture in the atmosphere favours the growth of mosses on bark (3a). In a drier environment, the same variety of birch is more ornamentally white (3b).

[3a]

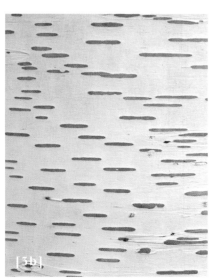

[3b]

[4a]

[4b]

Mosses proliferate on the bark of trees when there is a high annual rainfall and when dense planting prevents air from circulating freely. In this case it is strongly recommended to clean trunks every year in order to show their beauty to its best advantage.

For snakebark maples, for instance, use a microfibre cloth even if by doing so you remove some of the white bloom that covers them (1a). It will quickly reappear a few months later, especially at the end of winter (1b).

Less fragile bark (*Betula*, *Prunus* etc) can be cleaned with a high-pressure hose [2], or else with a sponge and water (3a, 3b), using Marseilles soap or white vinegar for more persistent stains. As you rub the bark fairly vigorously, its last strips may peel off naturally, particularly in birches (3c). Don't worry about this: energetic scrubbing doesn't harm the tree at all. Depending on the species, the layer of bark freshly exposed may show cream or orange tints which subsequently revert to their original white (3d).

With its handsome foliage and ability to carpet the ground rapidly, ivy can be attractive. Nevertheless its growth needs to be controlled in order to prevent it from colonizing trunks and allow birches to maintain their immaculate whiteness.

[1a]

[1b]

[2]

Avoid planting perennials or vigorous shrubs just in front of a fine coppiced specimen (4a). The aim is not to hide it in dense vegetation but to show it off against an attractive background (4b).

BETULA (BIRCH)

Elegant, undemanding, luminous and sensual, the birch is an intrinsic part of a beautiful winter garden. With all its nuances and subtleties, this tree has the richest range of bark colours.

[1]

Planted in groves, the white trunks of the Himalayan birch go excellently with coloured dogwoods.

(HARLOW CARR, ENGLAND)

A background of conifers sets off the architectural value of the birch.

(SIR HAROLD HILLIER GARDENS, ENGLAND)

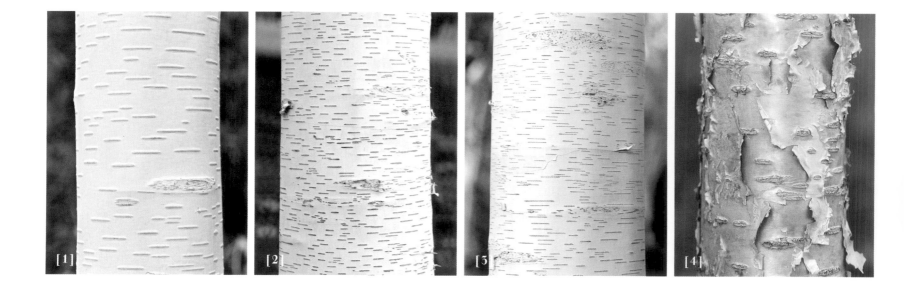

[1] [2] [3] [4]

To choose the right birch, take into account its shape, its size and the colour of its lenticels. The latter often fuse together to form decorative patches in low relief in *Betula ermanii* and its cultivars. On the contrary, they are usually narrow and elongated in *Betula albosinensis* and its cultivars.

PALE COLOURS

Striking and visible from a distance, the white or pastel-toned trunks of birches are equally effective when planted individually or in groups. Depending on the amount of rainfall, they can become covered in moss and thus lose their visual interest, so don't forget to clean them annually if need be.

From pure white to creamy white and pale yellow: *Betula utilis* var. *jacquemontii* 'Grayswood Ghost' [1] is one of the whitest cultivars, together with 'Trinity College' which has a very slender habit; *Betula forrestii* [2]; *Betula papyrifera* 'Saint Georges' [3] has very narrow lenticels; *Betula megrelica* [4] has a silvery metallic appearance; *Betula* 'Fetisowii' [5] has bark in deeper relief as if covered in layers of plaster; *Betula dahurica* [6] becomes silvery-grey as it ages; *Betula ermanii* 'Grayswood Hill' [7] is a magnificent birch with broad lenticels; *Betula alleghaniensis* [8] has unique golden tones.

The yellow birch, as if clothed in leaves of gold, shines out in the winter cold [8].
(ARNOLD ARBORETUM, USA)

BETULA (BIRCH)

WARM TINTS

Bark with brighter or deeper colours is valuable in groves where the trees are planted close together. It is shown off to its best advantage when mixed with trees with lighter trunks, the contrast giving rhythm to the planting. When planted individually, these birches gain from being grown as coppiced specimens.

From pale orange to pink to bright red:
Betula nigra 'Heritage' [1] has superb bark which, however, tends to darken after a few decades; *Betula albosinensis* [2] with its many named and coloured cultivars this birch is unbeatable in a winter garden; *Betula* 'Hergest' [3] keeps its orange colour in the shade but turns white if exposed to the sun; *Betula ermanii* 'Hakkoda Orange' and *Betula utilis* 'Nepalese Orange' are two more cultivars of interest for their handsome orange tints, as their names indicate; *Betula* 'Haywood' [4]; *Betula albosinensis* 'Princesse Sturdza' [5]; the attractive orange of *Betula albosinensis* 'Chinese Garden' [6] contrasts with the delicate golden colour revealed when the bark peels; the colour of *Betula albosinensis* Blason® 'Minrouge' [7] varies in intensity from year to year; *Betula* 'Lady in Red' [8] is the reddest of all birches.

Planted as a single specimen, the multi-trunked black birch is the key feature of this planting.

(L'ÉTANG DE LAUNAY, FRANCE)

[7]

Recent rain and the warm light of early evening bring out the orange colour of the trunks of *Betula albosinensis* var. *septentrionalis*.
(STONE LANE GARDENS, ENGLAND)

Chamaecyparis lawsoniana 'Rijnhof' forms an ideal backdrop for *Betula* 'Blason'.
(L'ÉTANG LE LAUNAY, FRANCE)

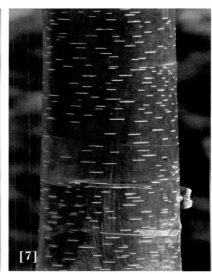

[5]

[6]

[7]

[8]

BETULA (BIRCH)

[1]

Set in a frame of light green, the birch cultivar
'Red Panda' is displayed to good effect.

(WISLEY, ENGLAND)

[6]

In a woodland setting the Himalayan birch cultivar 'Mount Luoji'
goes extremely well with varieties that have paler trunks.

(STONE LANE GARDENS, ENGLAND)

[1]

[2]

[5]

[4]

Together with the species *Betula gynoterminalis*,
the cultivar 'Park Wood' is the darkest birch.

DARKER TINTS

Light-coloured lenticels make wonderful pictorial
motifs that show even better on dark bark. When one
takes a closer look, trunks are true works of art.
To achieve a good contrast and a better readability of
the planting, give priority to combinations with other
white-trunked birches, with brambles whose stems
have a bloom on them, or with plants with light-
coloured foliage. With their characteristic straw colour,
grasses are ideal.

From brick red to chocolate to wine-red: *Betula
albosinensis* 'Red Panda' [1] has beautiful white
lenticels that look as if they have been applied with
a paintbrush and stand out from the mahogany-red
bark; *Betula utilis* 'Wakehurst Place Chocolate' [2]
shows all shades of chocolate; the broad bands of
prominent lenticels on *Betula ermanii* 'Mount Zao
Purple' [3] give it a striking striped appearance; *Betula
utilis* 'Bhutan Sienna' and *Betula albosinensis* 'Cacao'
[4] offer deep coppery-red hues; *Betula delavayi* [5];
Betula utilis 'Mount Luoji' [6]; *Betula gynoterminalis*
and *Betula utilis* 'Chris Lane' [7] are rarities unique for
the fineness of their bark and the delicate patterns of
their broad lenticels; *Betula utilis* 'Park Wood' [8] is a
magnificent wine-coloured cultivar that can become
almost black.

[5]

[6]

[7]

[8].

BETULA (BIRCH)

AUTUMN FOLIAGE

Some birch varieties offer more than simply their attractive bark. They can rival the most beautiful maples with foliage that changes colour in autumn. However, the range of colour is limited to the dominant shades of orange-yellow.

Betula papyrifera [1] has beautiful autumn colour although its bark is not the most spectacular; *Betula apoiensis* 'Mount Apoi' [2]; *Betula ermanii* [3] and its cultivars have it all: lovely bark of varied colours and notable autumn foliage; *Betula utilis* var. *jacquemontii* 'Jermyns' [4] in its handsome yellow garb. Other birches such as *Betula alleghaniensis*, *B. medwediewii*, *B. luminifera*, *B. dahurica* and the cultivar 'Fascination' are equally of interest. The amazing purple leaves of *Betula pendula* 'Royal Frost' and the creamy-white-variegated leaves of *Betula nigra* 'Shiloh Splash' both turn yellow in autumn.

(THE MANOR HOUSE, ENGLAND)

(BRESSINGHAM GARDENS, ENGLAND)

(JARDIN DU BOIS MARQUIS, FRANCE)

(JARDINS DE BELLEVUE, FRANCE)

(LAMBADER, FRANCE)

(JARDIN DU BOIS MARQUIS, FRANCE)

(JARDIN DU BOIS MARQUIS, FRANCE)

(WISLEY, ENGLAND)

SMALL BIRCHES

Betula ermanii is often of a small size and is thus ideal for small gardens. *Betula utilis* 'Long Trunk' [5] and *Betula nigra* 'Summer Cascade' have a weeping habit. *Betula medwediewii* 'Gold Bark' [6], *Betula megrelica* [7], *Betula nigra* 'Little King' [8], *Betula apoiensis* 'Mount Apoi' and *Betula* × *minor* 'Furlow' all have the charm of 'bonsai-type' birches and grow naturally as multi-trunked trees.

Seen against the light, the strips of peeling bark on *Betula albosinensis*
'Princesse Sturdza' seem to catch fire.

(LE CLOS DU VERBOSC, FRANCE)

RIGHT: The same light conditions are equally
spectacular for *Acer griseum*. Its fine translucent
bark catches the rays of the sun so that the
entire trunk and branches, down to the last
little twig, become fiery.

(SIR HAROLD HILLIER GARDENS, ENGLAND)

ACER (MAPLE)

Some maples have brightly coloured bark. They are visible from a distance but what is most striking is the beautiful detail of their 'snakeskin' bark. From close up one can make out the numerous veins, in a range of colours, which run across more or less pronounced lenticels.

[9]   [10]   [6]

(JARDINS DE BELLEVUE, FRANCE)   (LE VASTERIVAL, FRANCE)   (LE VASTERIVAL, FRANCE)

[1]   [2]   [3]   [4]

(JARDIN DU BOIS MARQUIS, FRANCE)

It is worth noting that these ornamental barks differ from those of birches or cherries. With a rare exception (*Acer griseum*), they do not peel. They are thus more prone to the growth of moss in regions where the rainfall is high.

COOL COLOURS

Shades of white: Whiteness depends on the production of bloom on trunks, which varies from season to season. *Acer tegmentosum* 'White Tigress' [9]; *Acer rufinerve* 'Green Star' [1]; *Acer davidii* 'Viper' [2] is one of the most beautiful *davidii* cultivars along with 'Rosalie'; *Acer tegmentosum* [3]; *Acer × conspicuum* 'Candy Stripe' [4] with its purplish veins; 'Valley Phantom' and 'Joe Witt' are recent cultivars of *Acer tegmentosum* which look very promising for the whiteness of their bark.

Shades of green: *Acer davidii* 'Rosalie' [5], very fast-growing, is the most interesting of the *davidii* cultivars, both for its foliage and for its bark, which can turn from emerald green to yellow-green during winter; *Acer × conspicuum* 'Silver Cardinal' [6] whose striking bark is clearly delineated into yellow and green areas; *Acer × conspicuum* 'Red Flamingo' [11] is similarly curious but has brighter red new shoots and even more interesting autumn foliage; the lozenge-shaped lenticels are prominent and well-formed in *Acer capillipes* and *Acer rubescens* [7]; *Acer laxiflorumn* [8]; *Acer pensylvanicum* 'Select' [10].

ACER (MAPLE)

AUTUMN FOLIAGE

All the maples selected for their fine bark have a major advantage: their leaves take on good colour in autumn, even if the colouring may sometimes vary from year to year. Together with *Acer capillipes* [7] and *Acer griseum*, *Acer laxiflorum* is among the species with the finest autumn colour, an intense orange-red. Cultivars of *Acer davidii* and *Acer tegmentosum* tend to turn yellow, but the most striking of the maples with yellow autumn foliage is *Acer × conspicuum* 'Phoenix' [8], whose butter-coloured leaves make a beautiful contrast with its pinkish trunk. Finally, let us not forget the variegated, speckled leaves of *Acer × conspicuum* 'Silver Cardinal', *Acer morifolium* 'Hime Yaku Nishiki' and above all of *Acer × conspicuum* 'Red Flamingo' [9] whose white variegation becomes pink while its green turns a luminous orange. Patience is required with *Acer × conspicuum* cultivars for they are capricious and hard to grow successfully.

(JARDIN DU BOIS MARQUIS, FRANCE)

(JARDIN DU BOIS MARQUIS, FRANCE)

(JARDIN DU BOIS MARQUIS, FRANCE)

WARM COLOURS

Shades of yellow: *Acer davidii* Bois Marquis selection [1] is distinguished by its very compact habit and bark that turns from green to orange-yellow in winter. Among the brighter yellows is *Acer rufinerve* 'Winter Gold' [2].

Shades of orange, pink and red: *Acer griseum* [3] has fine papery bark that peels in cinammon strips the same colour as the trunk; *Acer pensylvanicum* 'Erythrocladum' [4] has yellowish bark that turns more orange in winter; the green bark of *Acer pectinatum* 'Sirene' [5] becomes pink veined with fuchsia in winter; *Acer × conspicuum* 'Phoenix' [6] has orange bark that turns an almost fluorescent pinkish red in winter.

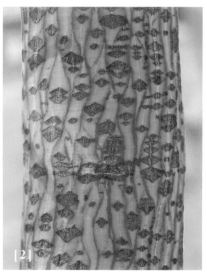

Simple, decorative and of the same
hue, grasses go very well with the
yellow bark of this maple.

(SIR HAROLD HILLIER GARDENS, ENGLAND)

A flamboyant planting of pink *Acer × conspicuum* 'Phoenix'
(in the foreground) and orange *Acer pensylvanicum*
'Erythrocladum' in a sea of blood-red dogwoods.

(JARDIN DU BOIS MARQUIS, FRANCE)

PRUNUS (CHERRY)

The name cherry might lead us to expect exuberant blossom in spring, but unfortunately we are not speaking here of the Japanese flowering cherries. Nevertheless, with their wonderful bark that peels in translucent strips these *Prunus* varieties are unbeatable in a winter garden.

Prunus serrula has shiny deep red bark with pink, purple or mahogany tints [4]. Its cultivar 'Branklyn' is a majestic large tree, unlike other *serrula* cultivars which are better adapted to small gardens.

(HARLOW CARR, ENGLAND)

Prunus himalaica: its numerous lenticels and dark colour resemble those of *Prunus rufa*, while its luminosity and mahogany-red are similar to those of *Prunus serrula* [5].

(WISLEY, ENGLAND)

Prunus maackii and its cultivars are excellent cherries during their early years. Unfortunately they do not age well and after fifteen years or so begin to decline and to lose their allure. The *Prunus maackii* type [1] is coppery red while the cultivars 'Amber Beauty' and especially 'Honey' [2] are more of a honey-orange colour. Among trees with amber-coloured bark the extremely rare Kumejima *Prunus* stands out from its competitors thanks to its profusion of deep pink single flowers.

Prunus serrula 'Jaro' is the most spectacular cherry.
Its smooth, fine bark shows different colours:
immediately after peeling it is olive green and then
quickly becomes orange-amber and mahogany [3].
(L'ÉTANG DE LAUNAY, FRANCE)

Prunus rufa (Hillier clone) is the darkest variety.
The regular, well-defined lenticels stand out against the
dominant wine and mahogany colours of the bark [6].
(L'ÉTANG DE LAUNAY, FRANCE)

PAPERY BARK

Depending on the species, papery barks peel every year to reveal a new skin, coming away in ragged strips which remain partially attached to the trunk or form thin sheets that accumulate over the years.

Decorative and colourful, the many tentacle-like branches of *Arbutus × andrachnoides* [6] enliven the garden in winter.

(JARDIN DU BOIS MARQUIS, FRANCE)

The reddish skin of *Arbutus menziesii* [7] splits into narrow strips to reveal the pistachio-green new bark.

(WESTERN CASCADE MOUNTAINS, OREGON, USA)

The shrubby *Arctostaphylos patula* [8]
has very delicate bark which forms curious
little rolls as it peels.
(CRATER LAKE NATIONAL PARK, OREGON, USA)

In full peeling, *Stewartia sinensis* [9]
changes its handsome pinkish bark to
a more classical greenish yellow.
(WAKEHURST PLACE, ENGLAND)

Arbutus × *andrachnoides* [6] and *Arbutus menziesii* [7], with its spectacular peeling and
generous spring flowering, make good alternatives. Also try *Arctostaphylos* [8]. No one
could fail to enjoy its decorative habit and wine-red bark. Three relatively hardy and
undemanding cultivars are *Arctostaphylos manzanita* 'Dr Hurd', *Arctostaphylos densiflora*
'Howard McMinn' and *Arctostaphylos* 'Austin Griffiths' which, like the cherry on the
cake, produces its small bunches of pink flowers throughout winter.
Stewartia sinensis [9] and *S. monadelpha* are real treasures, but patience is required as it
takes time for them to look their best.
Other curiosities worth trying are *Corylus fargesii* [1], whose bark resembles that of the
wonderful but tender *Fuchsia excorticata*; *Heptacodium miconioides* [2] with its typical
ragged strips of bark and scented autumn flowers; *Syringa pekinensis* 'China Snow' [3]
with its exceptionally shiny coppery bark; *Polylepis australis* [4] with countless layers of
amazing cinnamon-coloured bark; and various tree rhododendrons with unexpected bark
such as the cultivars 'Shilsonii' [5], 'Cornish Cross' and 'Mrs Kingsmill'.

PATCHY BARKS

Most deciduous trees with patchy bark are slow-growing. However, their attractive autumn foliage will help you be patient until you can fully enjoy their beautiful and colourful bark.

From its roots to the tips of its branches *Lagerstroemia* 'Osage' is covered in amber-coloured patches.

(THE US NATIONAL ARBORETUM, USA)

When it peels, *Myrtus luma* reveals white patches on its finely shredded orange bark. But beware, this plant is fairly tender.

(LOGAN BOTANIC GARDEN, SCOTLAND)

Stewartia pseudocamellia offers everything:
exquisite bark, luminous autumn foliage
and elegant flowers.

(GIARDINI BOTANICI DI VILLA TARANTO, ITALY)

When it sheds its bark *Pinus bungeana* shows
red patches on its grey-green camouflage uniform.

(DENVER BOTANIC GARDENS, USA)

Lagerstroemia is a small tree with a naturally architectural shape that is ideal in a winter
garden. In spite of the fact that its leaves do not turn red in autumn, the Japanese species
Lagerstroemia fauriei (1a) remains a model for trunks whose dominant colour is orange.
Many hybridizations of this species have given rise to superb cultivars such as 'Natchez',
'Kiowa', 'Osage' (1b) and 'Biloxi'. All of them have beautiful coloured bark, prolific summer
flowering, flamboyant autumn foliage and a great resistance to mildew.
In a small garden, allow yourself to be tempted by other striking species: *Cornus wilsoniana*
[2] whose bark recalls that of some Snow Gums; *Clethra barbinervis* [3] with scented
flowers in attractive colours in autumn; *Pseudocydonia sinensis* [4] which late in the year is
covered in quince-like fruit and scarlet foliage.
Among larger trees, *Zelkova sinica* [5] is incontestably the most majestic. When its bark
peels numerous orange patches appear on the trunk. *Ulmus parvifolia* and *Parrotia persica*
also have pleasant surprises in store, provided that you have acquired a good clone.

PATCHY BARK

The dark background of *Phormium tenax* sets off the
graceful habit of *Eucalyptus pauciflora* subsp. *debeuzevillei*
and its luminous branches delicately marbled with grey.

Moisture reveals and revives the colours
of *Eucalyptus subcrenulata*.

The hardiest *Eucalyptus* originating from the Snowy
Mountains of South-East Australia or the mountains and
high plateaux of Tasmania are suitable for winter gardens.
Eucalyptus pauciflora subsp. *debeuzevillei* [1] or subsp.
niphophila, *Eucalyptus gregsoniana* and *Eucalyptus coccifera*
are all Snow Gums with more or less light-coloured bark,
although in certain conditions the latter may take on
several colours. Other mountain species such as *Eucalyptus
stellulata* [2] or the amazing *Eucalyptus subcrenulata* [3]
develop more colourful trunks.

RIGHT: The ghostly *Eucalyptus pauciflora* subsp. *pauciflora*
has an unusually white trunk. It is the largest and the
most common of all Snow Gums.

CORNUS (DOGWOOD)

Coloured dogwoods are very vigorous suckering shrubs that are indispensable for winter gardens. Their stems offer a wide diversity of bright colours, from green to dark purple.

In very cold weather the fluorescent green stems of *Cornus sericea* 'Flaviramea' turn yellow at the same time as the bark of *Acer davidii* 'Rosalie'.

(JARDIN DU BOIS MARQUIS, FRANCE)

Cornus sanguinea 'Midwinter Fire' is a ball of yellow, orange and red flame which creates a marvellous contrast with the white trunks of birches.

(BRESSINGHAM GARDENS, ENGLAND)

Cornus sericea 'Flaviramea'

Cornus sanguinea 'Midwinter Fire'

Cornus sanguinea 'Magic Flame'

Cornus sanguinea 'Anny's Winter Orange'

With its fiery stems, *Cornus alba* 'Sibirica'
is ideal when planted in a small group to
brighten the darkest corners of the garden.

(JARDINS DE KERDALO, FRANCE)

Cornus alba 'Bâton Rouge'   *Cornus alba* 'Westonbirt'   *Cornus sericea* 'Baileyi'   *Cornus alba* 'Kesselringii'

CORNUS (DOGWOOD)

PRUNING AND ANNUAL GROWTH

Dogwoods require regular and severe pruning
to stimulate the growth of the brightly coloured
new stems. This coppicing or pollarding
unfortunately is at the cost of the flowers,
which are produced on the previous year's wood.

If your plant is vigorous, coppice it annually.
If it is slower-growing, leave the branches to
grow and cut them back only every two years.

When dealing with large plantings, start off
by reducing their size using a hedge-trimmer
or chain saw. Then finish off using secateurs,
cutting the stems to 5–7cm/2–3 inches from
the main trunk.

(JARDIN DU BOIS MARQUIS, FRANCE)

[1]

[2]

[1] These dogwoods were coppiced in early spring. For a few weeks this part of the garden will look a bit bare. Use plants that give structure (trunks, coloured evergreen foliage) in association with dogwoods to ensure a good transition between seasons after the dogwoods have been pruned.

[2] A month and a half later, nature is reasserting itself. New growth has once more covered a large part of the existing space.

[3] In autumn dogwoods take on colour one after the other. *Cornus alba* 'Westonbirt' opens the season, followed by *Cornus sanguinea* 'Magic Flame', in the foreground. The cultivar 'Winter Flame', in the background behind *Prunus serrula*, is the last in this series.

[4] Dogwood stems flame for at least four or five months. They make a brightly coloured spectacle which warms up even the darkest winter day.

[3]

[4]

CORNUS (DOGWOOD)

Leaf fall varies according to the cultivar: on the left
'Winter Flame' still holds its lovely autumn foliage,
while on the right 'Magic Flame' is already bare.
(JARDIN DU BOIS MARQUIS, FRANCE)

Cornus alba 'Aurea'   *Cornus sanguinea* 'Magic Flame'   *Cornus sanguinea* 'Winter Flame'   *Cornus alba* 'Kesselringii'

In autumn the fireworks begin with *Cornus alba* 'Sibirica'. A single specimen bears yellow, orange, pink, purple and red leaves.
(MARKS HALL GARDENS & ARBORETUM, ENGLAND)

Cornus alba 'Sibirica'   *Cornus alba* 'Sibirica Variegata'   *Cornus alba* 'Ivory Halo'   *Cornus sericea* 'Hedgerows Gold'

SALIX (WILLOW)

Used individually or in mass plantings, willows with coloured wood bring light to the garden. Their beauty is enhanced when set alongside a stream or beside a pond. Cut them back to the base every year in order to get fine splashes of colour.

[2]

[3]

(THE SAVILL GARDEN, ENGLAND)

[1]

[2]

[3]

[4]

(THE SAVILL GARDEN, ENGLAND)

WARM TONES

The most common colours are yellows and oranges with many nuances. *Salix alba* 'Jaune Hâtif' [1] is a slightly acid yellow and very luminous. *Salix alba* 'Golden Ness' [2] and 'Jaune de Falaise' are a good clear yellow with slightly amber tones.

For shades of orange there are three great classics: *Salix* × 'Erythroflexuosa' [3] with twisted branches, *Salix alba* 'Britzensis' [4], bright orange, and *Salix alba* 'Yelverton' [5] which is even more luminous, orange-yellow at its base and reddening at the tips of its branches. Blood red is a colour that does not exist in willows. The three cultivars that come nearest to it are *Salix alba* 'Flame Red' (with golden yellow autumn foliage), *Salix viminalis* 'Rouge Ardennais' [6] and *Salix alba* 'Liempde' [7] whose wood is a darker orange. The palette of warm colours ends with dark purple willows, often with decorative catkins in spring (*Salix daphnoides*) [8].

[5]

[6]

[7]

[8]

SALIX (WILLOW)

[1]

(JARDIN BOTANIQUE DE LA PRESLE, FRANCE)

[2]

(WISLEY, ENGLAND)

COOL TONES

Even if the bloom of the branches covers the stems more or less
uniformly in winter, white willows remain very ornamental.
The most outstanding are *Salix acutifolia* 'Lady Oldenham', *Salix
irrorata* [2] and *Salix acutifolia* 'Blue Streak', which has nuances
of violet-blue. *Salix myrsinifolia* [1], on the contrary, has attractive
deep black branches which contrast well with the orange stems
of other willows. *Salix cinerea* 'Olive Razetti' [3] is greyer but
still very striking as its wood is tomentose for a large part of the
winter before taking on an olive green hue. As far as shades of
green are concerned, *Salix arbuscula* [4] varies from khaki to olive
green, *Salix daphnoides* 'Green' [5] is a light green that borders
on the fluorescent, while the twisted stems of *Salix matsudana*
'Caradoc' are lime-green [6].

[1]

[2]

The uniform foreground of evergreens sets off the architectural
quality of *Salix babylonica* var. *pekinensis* 'Tortuosa'.
(HARLOW CARR, ENGLAND)

[3] [4] [5] [6]

ACER (MAPLE)

The so-called snakebark maples have ornamental bark over the whole tree. In other *Acer* species it is only the young branches that are striking, while the trunks cease to be of any interest as they age. After the warm colours of their autumn foliage, the bare stems in turn light up the garden.

Acer negundo 'Winter Lightning' [1] is very luminous. The current year's shoots, originally green, turn an almost fluorescent yellow as winter approaches.
(THE SAVILL GARDEN, ENGLAND)

Acer negundo var. *violaceum* [2] displays amazing violet-blue stems covered in a fine white bloom. In spring its pinkish-red flowers hang in elegant clusters.
(JARDIN DU BOIS MARQUIS, FRANCE)

Acer palmatum 'Bi Hoo' [4] is also worthy of note. Its finely cut leaves take on attractive colours over the seasons. The young shoots are orange-red (4a) then fade over time, while the orange-yellow of its old branches (4b) lasts for several years.
Acer palmatum 'Koto Hime' [5] is more curious. It is a naturally 'bonsai-type' maple whose greenish trunk has striking ringed markings.

The young, bright pink shoots of *Acer palmatum* 'Sango-kaku' [6] are dazzling throughout the winter. Just as exceptional is its cultivar 'Japanese Sunrise', whose branches veer between orange and red. The selection 'Eddisbury' [3] has redder wood but is less luminous. The cultivar 'Winter Flame' is ideal for small gardens.

(ANGLESEY ABBEY, ENGLAND)

(ÉTANG DE LAUNAY, FRANCE)

RUBUS (BRAMBLE)

In spite of their bad reputation, brambles have undeniable ornamental qualities which make them useful in winter gardens. Their striking and decorative habit can be seen from a distance. The stems spring from the ground like fountains, or are whip-like and harmoniously intertwined, giving rhythm and movement to the planting. To control their spread, keep an eye on them and prevent them from propagating naturally when the tips of the stems touch the soil.

(CAMBRIDGE UNIVERSITY BOTANIC GARDEN, ENGLAND)

(WISLEY, ENGLAND)

SHADES OF ORANGE-RED

The new shoots of *Rubus niveus* [1] are covered in downy hairs which are rapidly shed to reveal shiny mahogany-coloured thorny stems, reminiscent of the bark of the Tibetan cherry. *Rubus coreanus* 'Dart's Mahogany' offers darker wine-red colours. The reddish scapes of *Rubus phoenicolasius* [2] are covered with tiny silky hairs that catch the slightest ray of sunlight, making the stems glow so that they form beautiful luminous arches. This bramble is also prized for its sweet blackberries.

[5]

(ARBORETUM DE KALMTHOUT, BELGIUM)

SHADES OF WHITE

The regular, arching stems of *Rubus cockburnianus* [3] are covered with a white bloom, which reveals a delicate pink colour when it fades, particularly at the tips. *Rubus cockburnianus* 'Goldenvale' is distinguished by its handsome golden foliage in summer and by a more compact habit. The undulating stems flow over the ground like waves. It is slower-growing and less invasive than other varieties of *Rubus*.

The downy, grey-green, finely cut leaves of *Rubus thibetcnus* [4] are reminiscent of a heather, but the white bloom does not last as long as that on other brambles.

The large, broad, naturally arching canes of *Rubus lasiostylus* var. *hubeiensis* [5] are armed with a multitude of small thorns. Its habit is regular and graceful and its white bloom lasts all winter. It is the most majestic of the white brambles.

The bloom on *Rubus biflorus* [6] covers all the stems, which are initially green and equipped with a few large conical thorns. Together with *Rubus lasiostylus*, this is without doubt the whitest bramble. Its rampant habit leads it to snake away in all directions.

[5] [4] [5] [6]

BAMBOOS

Many gardeners are passionate about the colouration of bamboo culms. It is, however, a complex subject: the colours vary a lot depending on exposure (all bamboos go yellow in the sun), rainfall, age, soil, the amount of bloom on the plant, the difference in temperature between day and night, and of course the species.

Phyllostachys species always enliven and light up the garden, regardless of whether they are grey-blue (*Phyllostachys nigra* f. *henonis*), tender green (*Phyllostachys viridiglaucescens*) or shades of gold (*Phyllostachys aureosulcata* f. *aureocaulis* on the left and *Phyllostachys vivax* f. *aureocaulis* on the right).

(BAMBOUSERAIE EN CÉVENNES, FRANCE)

[1] [2] [5] [4]

The variegated foliage of *Phyllostachys edulis* 'Okina' has a rare beauty. *Phyllostachys aurea* 'Eyragues' is easier to grow and is also very luminous.
(BAMBOUSERAIE EN CÉVENNES, FRANCE)

The blueish bloom on its young canes makes *Thamnocalamus crassinodus* 'Kew Beauty' extremely decorative.
(ROSEMOOR, ENGLAND)

BLACK: The turions of *Phyllostachys nigra* [1] are green when they emerge, then gradually become darker to turn into completely black culms after two or three years. The form f. *nigra* has an exceptional colour, while cultivars of *Phyllostachys nigra* such as 'Addington' and 'Othello' seem to turn black more quickly if all the right conditions are met.

YELLOW AND ORANGE: Depending on the plants' exposure to the sun, the nuances of yellow range from golden to reddish-orange. *Phyllostachys bambusoides* 'Holochrysa' is without doubt one of the most beautiful orange-yellow bamboos. Easy to grow and decorative, *Phyllostachys aureosulcata* and its varieties are great classics that are highly effective at lighting up the garden in winter.

The internodes are covered with thousands of tiny crystals which catch and reflect the light and which make them rough to the touch. The yellow turions of *Phyllostachys aureosulcata* f. *aureocaulis* [2] turn red as they drink in the sun but later regain their definitive golden colour. The form f. *lama tempel* [3] is a fine, clear and luminous yellow. For gardeners who are impatient and like yellow canes with large diameters, *Phyllostachys vivax* f. *aureocaulis* is a remarkable giant which, however, does not age well. It breaks easily and becomes soiled.

GREEN AND BLUE: *Phyllostachys edulis* remains unbeatable, but newly introduced plants such as *Phyllostachys prominens* [4] are equally worthwhile. With prominent nodes, impressive enamelled green culms and the ability to attain

a good diameter rapidly, it is one of the finest bamboos currently in cultivation.
In some bamboos, the young canes are covered in a layer of more or less blue bloom, rarely lasting longer than a year. This characteristic is clearly seen in *Fargesia albocerea* and *Fargesia papyrifera*, both of which unfortunately are tender. Much hardier is *Thamnocalamus crassinodus* 'Kew Beauty', a marvel which likes to have its feet dry in winter, or *Phyllostachys glauca* which requires patience before its fine blue appearance can be enjoyed.

UNUSUAL BAMBOOS

Bamboos can take the gardener, amateur and expert alike, by surprise.
Some of them produce highly curious culms, while others are spotted
or striped as if painted.

The curious *Phyllostachys edulis*
'Heterocycla', known in Japan as 'Kikko',
calls to mind the carapace of a tortoise.
Another surprising form is f. *tubaeformis*.

(BAMBOUSERAIE EN CÉVENNES, FRANCE)

For beginners, *Phyllostachys aurea*
'Holochrysa' is less rare and a lot easier
to succeed with than Kikko.

(BAMBOUSERAIE EN CÉVENNES, FRANCE)

Known for its swollen cymbal-like nodes,
Chimonobambusa tumidissinoda was used to
make Charlie Chaplin's famous cane.

(BAMBOUS EN PROVENCE, FRANCE)

All varieties of *Phyllostachys aureosulcata* have varyingly pronounced zigzags in their canes. The form *spectabilis* is a good example.

(JARDIN DU BOIS MARQUIS, FRANCE)

SPOTTED AND STRIPED PATTERNS

After a few years *Phyllostachys bambusoides* f. *tanakae* [1] develops wonderfully decorative blotches on its green culms that last over time. In *Phyllostachys nigra* 'Boryana' and *Phyllostachys glauca* f. *yunzhu* the blotches fade, becoming more like faint haloes. In both *Phyllostachys bambusoides* f. *lacrima-deae* and the striking *Phyllostachys bambusoides* f. *mixta* [2], which after 4–5 years becomes completely black with a fluorescent yellow groove, the blotches tend to spread into a uniform colour.

Other *Phyllostachys* varieties have very decorative coloured stripes. These brush strokes are mostly yellow or green, are of very variable breadth and are distributed more or less evenly over the culms. *Phyllostachys bambusoides* 'Castillonis Inversa', *Phyllostachys vivax* f. *huangwenzhu* [3] and *Phyllostachys iridescens* are good representatives of the category of green bamboos with yellow stripes. In the extremely rare *Phyllostachys nigra* f. *mejiro*, the contrast between the yellow groove and the deep black stem is striking.

Yellow culms striped with green stand out better in the garden, being more luminous and having a greater diversity of patterns. *Phyllostachys vivax* f. *huangwenzhu inversa* is one of the most beautiful in this group. Like all forms of *Phyllostachys vivax*, it grows fast and very rapidly develops canes with a large diameter but little density. The reverse side of the coin is that these canes are often broken by the wind or under the weight of snow. They also easily become soiled. *Phyllostachys edulis* and its varieties are sumptuous bamboos which improve with age but are hard to grow. With its graceful habit, small leaves and finely drawn stripes, *Phyllostachys edulis* f. *nabeshimana* [4] is without doubt one of the most refined bamboos, closely followed by *Phyllostachys aureosulcata* f. *flavostriata* [5]. Its exquisite cinnamon-coloured canes and delicate leaves make *Phyllostachys edulis* 'Bicolor' [6] a must for experienced bamboo enthusiasts. With its reduced internodes and its broad green stripe, *Phyllostachys praecox* f. *viridisulcata* [7] is also an attractive curiosity. *Phyllostachys sulphurea* 'Robert Young' and *Phyllostachys bambusoides* 'Castillonis' complete this wonderfully artistic palette of bamboos.

[4] [5] [6] [7]

BERBERIS, FRAXINUS, TILIA, ETC.

There are a few more curiosities that complete the already rich palette of plants with coloured wood; they brighten gardens not only in winter but in autumn too, as well as during their different flowering periods.

The young shoots of *Berberis dictyophylla* are covered in a fine white bloom which gives them a frosted look throughout the winter.

(JARDIN DU BOIS MARQUIS, FRANCE)

Fraxinus excelsior 'Jaspidea' seems to like yellow: this is the colour of its very decorative strong branches in winter, as well as of both its spring and its autumn foliage.

(JARDIN DU BOIS MARQUIS, FRANCE)

Graceful and elegant, *Kolkwitzia amabilis* 'Pink Cloud' lights up the garden with its profuse pink flowers and its characteristically papery white bark.

(JARDIN DE LA BUISSONNIÈRE, FRANCE)

Tilia cordata 'Winter Orange' has more than one asset: sweetly scented flowers, golden autumn foliage and orange-coloured young stems.

(WISLEY, ENGLAND)

For shades of green, why not try a handsome clump of *Equisetum camtschatcense* [1]? This giant horsetail has highly decorative upright stems and is just as refined and Japanese-looking as a bamboo. However, it is invasive and you therefore need to keep an eye on it. The young branches of *Tilia platyphyllos* 'Aurea' [2] are a more acid green. *Styphnolobium japonicum*, has some very interesting cultivars with yellow wood, such as 'Winter Gold'. The cultivar 'Flavirameum' [3] tends towards an intense acid yellow, whereas 'Gold Standard' [4] is more of a golden yellow. In autumn their leaves light up like the sun. Black is always a surprising colour and difficult to handle in the garden, but the dry round flower heads of *Hydrangea macrophylla* 'Nigra' [5] provide a good foil for its ebony stems. The more vigorous cultivar 'Zorro' is distinguished by its flattened inflorescences.

(HARLOW CARR, ENGLAND)

OTHER TOUCHES OF COLOUR

Bark shouldn't be the only source of colour in the garden in winter. Flowers, fruits and evergreen foliage, often very colourful, also have a part to play. It is important to add colour in different ways, not limiting it to linear forms such as trunks and stems but rather adding small, delicate touches as in an impressionist painting.

WINTER-FLOWERING TREES AND SHRUBS

Flowers that brave the cold are subtle, luminous and often strongly scented. At this time of year pollinators are few and far between, and so plants have to do everything they can to attract them. The plants described here mostly bloom in the winter months when gardeners have the greatest need of colour and scent as they await the fine days of spring.

Hamamelis × *intermedia* 'Arnold Promise' spreads its flower-laden branches in a winter scene already given colour by flaming stems.
(ÉTANG DE LAUNAY, FRANCE).

Hamamelis and its hybrids are the kings of winter. In spite of the icy cold they open their curiously spider-like flowers, formed of slightly crumpled petals, which light up in the faintest ray of sunlight. RIGHT: Thanks to the work of Robert and Jelena de Belder among others, there are a great many Sino-Japanese hybrids (× *intermedia*) that often have very fragrant flowers and fabulous autumn colour.

TOP: In bud from the autumn, *Stachyurus praecox* has delicate hanging clusters of flowers that wait patiently for fine weather to open. *Stachyurus chinensis*, less tender, has more impressive flowers but they open even later. ABOVE: Amidst colourful stems, the flowers of *Viburnum × bodnantense* 'Charles Lamont' provide perfume throughout the winter.

LEFT: *Daphne bholua* 'Jacqueline Postill' [1] is slightly tender but produces a profusion of flowers with an intoxicating fragrance in all shades of pink; *Sarcococca confusa* [2] is an unbeatable small shrub with a pervasive scent; *Prunus mume* 'Beni Chidori' [3] has scented deep pink double flowers; *Skimmia japonica* is indispensable for its coloured buds in winter and its scented white flowers in spring, followed by numerous red berries. The cultivar 'Magic Marlot' [4] has handsome variegated foliage; the silky buds of *Edgeworthia chrysantha* are held on the plant all winter before opening into scented flowers that are yellow in the cultivar 'Grandiflora' [5] and more orange in 'Red Dragon' [7]; *Mahonia × media* 'Buckland' [6] has golden yellow flowers with a sweet lily of the valley scent from autumn onwards, as well as evergreen foliage that sometimes turns red in cold weather; the translucent yellow flowers of *Chimonanthus praecox* [8] with their spicy scent appear only on plants that have attained a certain age.

Heathers create rhythm by adding volume and colour. They make a perfect groundcover and serve as a harmonious link between coloured stems, bark and dwarf conifers or even grasses. *Erica carnea* and one of its hybrids, *Erica × darleyensis*, stand out. They have given rise to numerous hardy cultivars, easy to grow even in slightly alkaline soil, which produce a profusion of flowers, often scented, over a long period – at least for all the winter. Some cultivars increase this festival of colour with their ornamental foliage – coppery ('Ann Sparkes') or lime-green ('Golden Starlet').

WINTER-FLOWERING PERENNIALS AND BULBS

These delicate flowers look so fragile and yet bravely withstand the icy cold to offer an incredible symphony of colours. Winter-flowering perennials and bulbs are a real asset to beautify the dullest of beds.

Hellebore flowers, particularly those of *orientalis* hybrids, offer an amazing range of colours. Give priority to pastel shades as they are more easily visible even though, individually, some dark reds and purples ('Anna's Red', for example) are extremely beautiful.
(JARDINS DE BELLEVUE, FRANCE)

RIGHT: In autumn, *Helleborus niger* is always the first to flower. The cultivar 'Potter's Wheel' is a must. Once these have finished, *Helleborus orientalis* takes over until spring. Recently, Martine Lemonnier succeeded in the much desired hybridization of these two species, giving rise to the star of the winter, *Helleborus × lemonnierae* [2]. It has an exceptionally long flowering period, with the flowers opening pale pink in late autumn and finishing carmine red in mid-spring. With their clusters of pale yellow and acid green flowers, *Helleborus argutifolius* [1] and *Helleborus foetidus* [3] shine out: in early-flowering *Crocus* species various colours are seen: mauve for *Crocus tommasinianus* [4], golden for *Crocus ancyrensis* 'Golden Bunch' and white for *Crocus tommasinianus* f. *albus*; *Galanthus caucasicus* [5], along with a great many other snowdrops, and *Leucojum vernum* emerge from the snow without the slightest difficulty; dwarf irises stand out for their amazing shades of blue: from sky blue in *Iris* 'Katharine Hodgkin' [6] to sapphire in 'Harmony'; carpeting the ground beneath trees, the golden yellow buds of *Eranthis hyemalis* [7] and the delicate petals of *Cyclamen coum* [8] in shades of pink light up even the smallest area.

BERRIES AND FLESHY FRUITS

Evergreen foliage makes coloured fruits stand out, but the pictorial effect is even more spectacular on bare branches or stems. These titbits are a feast for birds, which unfortunately sometimes devour them all too fast as winter approaches.

Against a background of birches with snow-white trunks, the small scarlet apples of *Malus* 'Evereste' remind us of the magic of Christmas.

(WEST GREEN HOUSE GARDEN, ENGLAND)

RIGHT: *Sorbus sargentiana* [1]: with their flamboyant autumn leaves and many-coloured berries, rowans end the year on a note of beauty; ornamental apple trees are interesting at every season. The red fruits of *Malus* 'Red Jewel' [2] last, incredibly, throughout the whole winter. *Malus transitoria* [3] and the cultivars 'Jean-Pierre Hennebelle', 'Golden Hornet', 'Indian Magic', *Malus coronaria* 'Crittenden' [8] and 'Nicolas Hennebelle' [6] continue to hold their fruits fairly well after the end of autumn; in spite of its tenderness, *Melia azedarach* [4] deserves a place of honour for its fruits which last intact on the tree for at least six months; as soon as its leaves have fallen, *Idesia polycarpa* [5] shows off its attractive clusters of small red pea-like fruits; *Diospyros kaki* [7] is a magical sight as Christmas approaches, an edible as well as a visual pleasure.

LEFT: *Rosa* 'Splendens' [1] has large red hips and a scent of myrrh; *Ilex aquifolium* 'Pyramidalis Fructu Luteo' [2], which has yellow berries, and the very fructiferous *Ilex × altaclerensis* 'Lawsoniana' [3], which has elegant variegated foliage, are evergreen hollies that are always effective. The bare branches of *Ilex verticillata* and its hybrids such as 'Sparkleberry' are weighed down by their red berries; the pure white berries of *Skimmia japonica* 'Wakehurst White' [4] stand out against the shiny leaves; *Celastrus rosthornianus* [5] produces blazing red seeds in orange-yellow capsules; *Nandina domestica* 'Richmond' [6] has coloured foliage throughout the year and abundant fruits in winter; in spite of the fact that × *Didrangea versicolor* [7] is tender, the unique blue colour of its berries makes it a temptation to gardeners; the scarlet fruits of *Berberis* 'Georgei' [8] rival its yellow flowers and its handsome autumn foliage.

The unique lilac-coloured berries of *Callicarpa dichotoma* go extremely well with any coppiced white-trunked birches. The cultivar 'Profusion' is exceptional.

(ARBORETUM DE WESPELAAR, BELGIUM)

DRY INFLORESCENCES AND FRUITS

The inflorescences of many perennials and some shrubs dry out to become
very decorative, with colours ranging from pearly white or straw yellow to
dark brown or black.

In the gardens of The Manor House and Hyde Hall,
the long, graceful panicles of *Cortaderia* and the angel's
hair of *Stipa* species bring rhythm, lightness and light
to winter plantings.

RIGHT: The small fruits of *Cotinus coggygria* f. *purpureus* [1] are surrounded by clouds of feathery plumes;
after their prolific mauve flowers in autumn, the black stems of *Aster* sp. [2] develop handsome tufts
of golden achenes; *Lunaria rediviva* [3] is a superb Honesty, withstanding wind and snow and bearing
decorative mother of pearl seed pods; the yellow flowers arranged in tiers around the stems of *Phlomis
russeliana* [4] dry out and turn black in winter; *Sedum spectabile* [5] flowers prolifically from summer into
autumn, after which its dry inflorescences take on shades of copper, brown and black; *Cortaderia selloana*
'Aureolineata' [6] has graceful flowering stems and a clump of very luminous acid yellow-green leaves;
Miscanthus nepalensis [7] and *Miscanthus sinensis* 'Grosse Fontäne' [8] make beautiful plumes.

LEFT: Once they have faded, the sepals of *Hydrangea* species remain on the stem and take on an attractive pale straw colour. They go very well with all kinds of bark, especially with the red stems of *Cornus alba* 'Westonbirt'.

TOP: To catch the low rays of the sun and light up the garden in winter, choose hydrangeas with substantial flower heads such as this *Hydrangea arborescens* 'Annabelle' in the Jardin du Perdier or some cultivars of *Hydrangea paniculata*.

ABOVE: Grasses also give a spectacular effect when they form beautiful plumes like *Miscanthus sinensis* 'Gracillimus' and 'Malepartus'. The Botanic Garden of La Presle offers a wonderful scene with many cultivars of *Miscanthus sinensis* such as 'Krater', 'Kleine Silberspinne', 'Silberfeder' and 'Grosse Fontäne'.

AMAZING CONIFERS

Whether they are large or dwarf, columnar or spreading, conifers are outstanding in winter gardens. Concentrate on those which change colour with the first frosts, although the classic blue hues are also always spectacular.

Against the blue background of *Abies procera* 'Glauca', *Pinus sylvestris* 'Gold Medal' turns from green to golden at the end of autumn.
(JARDIN DU BOIS MARQUIS, FRANCE).

RIGHT: All the conifers on this page have foliage that is initially green but changes colour in winter.

COPPERY TONES: *Podocarpus* 'County Park Fire' [1], *Cryptomeria japonica* 'Elegans' [2], the excellent groundcover *Microbiota decussata* [3] and its variegated cultivar 'Gold Spot'.

PURPLE TONES: *Platycladus orientalis* takes on the incredible plum colours also seen in the cultivar 'Juniperoides' [5], as well as in 'Rosedalis', 'Meldensis' and 'Sanderi'.

GOLDEN TONES: *Pinus mugo* 'Ophir' [4] or 'Winter Gold', *Pinus contorta* 'Chief Joseph' [7], *Pinus wallichiana* 'Winter Light' and *Pinus sylvestris* 'Gold Medal' are excellent pines which turn gold in winter. *Abies nordmanniana* 'Golden Spreader' [6] and *Calocedrus decurrens* 'Berrima Gold' [8] are also fine specimens with yellow winter foliage.

[1]

[2]

[3]

[4]

[5]

[6]

[7]

[8]

[1]

[2]

[3]

[4]

[5]

[6]

Powdered with hoar frost or snow, topiaries of *Taxus baccata*
can bring a touch of magic to the garden.

(ÉTANG DE LAUNAY, FRANCE)

LEFT: The palette of conifers today is extraordinarily rich. Some of these trees develop very unusual
habits. *Metasequoia glyptostroboides* [1] is one of the rare deciduous conifers with superb autumn colour
whose trunk becomes curiously furrowed and swollen at the base; *Sequoiadendron giganteum* 'Pendulum'
[2] has a strange silhouette that makes winter even more mysterious; *Cedrus atlantica* 'Glauca Pendula'
[3] has an almost ghostly weeping habit; *Araucaria araucana* [4] has a conical shape with branches in
very regular tiers, which with age become a high dome at the top; *Taxus baccata* 'Fastigiata Aurea' [5]:
used as 'sentinels' in the Jardins de Séricourt, these columnar yews add powerful emotion to the
composition; *Picea omorika* 'Pendula Bruns' [6] has short, dense, weeping branches that create a natural
sculpture in the style of Giacometti.

OTHER EVERGREENS WITH WINTER COLOUR

Cold has a seemingly magical power over the foliage of some evergreens,
be they groundcovers, perennials or shrubs: the chlorophyll in their leaves
is replaced by anthocyanins and other brightly coloured pigments.

In winter *Bergenia* 'Bressingham Ruby'
carpets the soil and warms the atmosphere
like a flow of lava.
(BRESSINGHAM GARDENS, ENGLAND)

FOLLOWING DOUBLE PAGE: SIR HAROLD HILLIER GARDENS, ENGLAND

RIGHT: Starting off green, all the evergreens
on this page take on amazing colours in
winter. *Leucothoe fontanesiana* 'Rainbow'
[1] and the cultivar *Lecothoe keiskei* 'Royal
Ruby' offer attractive shades of red;
the superb multicoloured hues of *Euonymus
fortunei* 'Emerald 'n' Gold' [2] are outlined
by frost; *Bergenia* 'Bressingham Ruby' [3]
is an excellent groundcover whose foliage
turns beetroot-red, as does that of *Bergenia
purpurascens*; *Mahonia bealei* [4], often
confused with its close relative *Mahonia
japonica*, has striking autumn foliage in
the depths of winter; *Mahonia aquifolium*
'Atropurpureum' turns purple whereas its
cultivar 'Apollo' [5] becomes almost black;
Libertia peregrinans 'Gold Leaf' [6] forms
a handsome clump of orange-yellow leaves;
Calluna vulgaris 'Golden Feather' [7] is one
of the many heathers which takes on an
orange colour; *Hakonechloa macra* 'Nicolas'
[8] is a ball of fire in autumn whose colour
fades in winter but still maintains attractive
traces of its brilliance.

INDEX

For gardeners in the UK, the website of the Royal Horticultural Society (www.rhs.org.uk/Plants) provides information on plant suppliers. Simply type in the exact name of the plant you are looking for and you will find a list of the nurseries in the UK that stock it.

FOR PLANTS WITH ATTRACTIVE BARK AND MUCH ELSE:

UK
- Beeches Nursery, Essex
- Bluebell Aboretum & Nursery, Derbyshire
- Hergest Croft Gardens, Herefordshire
- JPR Environmental, Gloucestershire
- Junker's Nursery, Somerset
- Pan-Global Plants, Gloucestershire
- Stone Lane Garden Tree nursery, Devon
- Thornayes Nursery, Devon
- Whitelea Nursery, Derbyshire

France
- Les Botaniques du Val d'Ouve à Saint-Sauveur-le-Vicomte
- Le Clos du Verbosc, Touffreville-la-Corbeline
- La Grange aux Érables, Montvendre
- Pépinière Brochet-Lanvin, Nanteuil-la-Forêt
- Pépinière Christian Bessard, Polliat
- Pépinière Hennebelle, Boubers-Sur-Canche
- Pépinière Maurice Laurent, Saint-Romain-en-Gal
- Pépinière Philippe Leclercq, Hantay
- Un Jardin au Mont-Blanc, Domancy

FOR BAMBOOS:

UK
- Larch Cottage Nurseries, Cumbria
- Norfolk Bamboo Company, Norfolk

France
- Bambous de Planbuisson, Buisson-de-Cadouin
- Bambouseraie en Cévennes, Générargues
- Newfi Bamboo, Luzillat
- Pépinières de Créa'Paysage, Ploemeur

USA
- Song Sparrow Nursery, WI

FOR WINTER-FLOWERING PLANTS, AMONG OTHER NURSERIES:

UK
- RHS Garden Wisley, Surrey
- Witch Hazel Nursery, Kent

France
- Pépinière Botanique, Gaujacq
- Pépinières Cavatore, Bormes-les-Mimosas
- Pépinières Dauguet, Larchamp
- Pépinières Delabroye, Hantay

- Pépinières Delay, Vienne
- Pépinière Ellebore, Saint-Jouin-de-Blavou
- Pépinière du Jardin de Bellevue, Beaumont-le-Hareng
- Pépinières Roué, Plouigneau
- Promesse de fleurs, Houplines

USA
- Garden Crossings, MI
- Plant Delights, NC

FOR CONIFERS, AMONG OTHER NURSERIES:

UK
- Acorn Trees and Shrubs, Devon
- Kenwith Conifer Nursery, Devon
- Larch Cottage Nurseries, Cumbria
- Lime Cross Nursery, East Sussex

France
- Atypique Flore, Saint-André-Le-Bouchoux
- Pépinières Botaniques Armoricaines, Saint-Adrien
- Pépinière Botanique des Montagnes Noires, Spézet
- Pépinières des Laurains, Viâpres-le-Petit

USA
- Rare Find Nursery, NJ

FOR GRASSES:

UK
- Knoll Gardens, Dorset
- Pan-Global Plants, Gloucestershire

France
- Bambous de Planbuisson, Buisson-de-Cadouin
- Pépinières de Créa'Paysage, Ploemeur
- Pépinière du Jardin Plume, Auzouville-sur-Ry
- Pépinières Lumen, Creysse
- Pépinière Le jardin d'herbes, Bazouges-la-Pérouse

USA
- Digging Dog Nursery, CA

OTHER US NURSERIES:

- Forest Farm Nursery, OR
- Prairie Nursery, WI
- Laporte Avenue Nursery, CO
- Florida Native Plant Nursery, FL
- Hill Country Natives, TX

GARDENS

ILLUSTRATED IN THIS BOOK

Many of the gardens in this list welcome visitors. Information on their opening hours can easily be found on the Internet. The gardens listed as private may occasionally be visited, but always by appointment only.

FRANCE
- Bambouseraie en Cévennes, Générargues
- Bambous en Provence, Eyragues
- Jardin All Zen, Luzillat
  Private garden, visits by appointment only
- Jardin Botanique de la Presle, Nanteuil-la-Forêt
- Jardin Botanique de l'Université de Strasbourg, Strasbourg
- Jardins de Bellevue, Beaumont-le-Hareng
- Jardin de La Buissonnière, Taluyers
  Private garden, visits by appointment only
- Jardins de l'École du Breuil, Paris
- Jardins de Séricourt, Séricourt
- Jardin du Bois Marquis, Vernioz
- Jardin des Closeraies, Tauxières-Mutry
- Jardins de Kerdalo, Trédarzec
- Jardin de Valérianes, Bosc-Roger-sur-Buchy
- La Bizerie, Saint-Maurice-en-Cotentin
- La Mare aux Trembles, Épreville-près-le-Neubourg
  Private garden, visits by appointment only
- Lambader, Plouvorn
  Private garden, visits by appointment only
- La Pommeraie, Saint-Nicolas-d'Aliermont
  Private garden
- Le Clos du Verbosc, Touffreville-la-Corbeline
  Private garden, visits by appointment only
- Le Perdrier, Sucé-sur-Erdre
  Private garden, visits by appointment only
- Les Bambous du Mandarin, Montauroux
- L'Étang de Launay, Varengeville-sur-Mer
  Private garden, visits by appointment only
- Le Vasterival, Sainte-Marguerite-sur-Mer
- Parc de la Tête d'Or, Lyon
- Pépinières Botaniques de Cambremer, Cambremer
- Pépinière Jean-Pierre Hennebelle, Boubers-sur-Canche
- Pépinières Minier, Beaufort-en-Vallée
  Private arboretum

ENGLAND
- Anglesey Abbey, Lode
- Bressingham Gardens, Diss
- Cambridge University Botanic Garden, Cambridge
- Hergest Croft Gardens, Kington
- Kew Royal Botanic Gardens, Richmond
- Lady Farm Gardens, Chelwood
  Private garden, visits by appointment only
- Marks Hall Gardens & Arboretum, Coggeshall
- RHS Garden Harlow Carr, Harrogate
- RHS Garden Hyde Hall, Chelmsford
- RHS Garden Rosemoor, Torrington
- RHS Garden Wisley, Woking
- Sir Harold Hillier Gardens, Romsey
- Stone Lane Gardens, Chagford
- The Manor House, Stevington
- The Savill Garden, Englefield Green
- Wakehurst Place, Ardingly
- West Green House Gardens, Hartley Wintney
- Westonbirt Arboretum, Tetbury

SCOTLAND
- Logan Botanic Garden, Port Logan
- Royal Botanic Garden Edinburgh, Edinburgh

ITALY
- Giardini Botanici di Villa Taranto, Pallanza

BELGIUM
- Arboretum de Kalmthout, Kalmthout
- Arboretum Wespelaar, Wespelaar
- Domaine d'Hemelrijk, Essen
  Private garden, visits by appointment only

UNITED STATES
- The Arnold Arboretum of Harvard University, Boston
- The United States National Arboretum, Washington
- Crater Lake National Park, Oregon
- Denver Botanic Gardens, Denver
- Aspen Forest, Colorado
- Western Cascade Mountains, Oregon

ACKNOWLEDGMENTS

Behind every garden is a gardener. Without these men and women none of the explosions of colour that have inspired me, winter after winter, would exist. This book gives me the opportunity to pay homage to them, perhaps at the same time even enabling them to see their gardens through the eyes of another plant lover. All these passionate, visionary and bold gardeners generously gave me access to the paradises that they have created. I thank them from the bottom of my heart. To three of them, Christian Peyron, Jean-Louis Dantec and Jérôme Goutier, I owe special gratitude for the way they inspired me, supported me and contributed to the success of my project.

I am also extremely grateful to the team at Éditions Ulmer and in particular to Antoine Isambert, its Director, who was always enthusiastic and ready to listen to me, respecting my choices and efforts. Without such a relationship of trust this book would not have seen the light of day.

I should like to express my profound thanks to my family and close friends who have always given me unconditional support. For me this book is an act of homage to my roots and above all to my parents; they instilled in me values which I hope to pass on, humbly and sensitively, through the way I look at and photograph these gardens.

It took me nine years to produce this book. I needed to carry out research, to discover the most beautiful winter gardens, to study them and photograph them at different times under harsh winter conditions – harsh indeed for a southerner like myself, more accustomed to a warm climate. All the people mentioned above gave me courage, optimism and the energy to surmount difficulties and to complete my work on plants with beautiful bark. And now, free of spirit and light of heart, I can turn over a new page and henceforth devote myself to other equally fascinating botanical subjects.

PHOTOGRAPHY CREDITS

All photographs by Cédric Pollet
www.cedric-pollet.com

apart from the following:
- Adrian Bloom: Foggy Bottom, Bressingham Gardens, p. 10.

- Patrick Murray: *Eucalyptus coccifera*, p. 143.

- Christian Monnet: *Betula gynoterminalis*, p. 146 and *Eucalyptus subcrenulata*, p. 172.

- Alex Bachelet: *Betula albosinensis* 'Cacao', p. 156.

- Franck Sadrin: *Betula utilis* 'Chris Lane', p. 157.

- Mark Dwyer: *Syringa pekinensis* 'China Snow', p. 168.

- Wayne M. Paquette: *Platycladus orientalis* 'Juniperoides', p. 213.

Winter Gardens
Text copyright © Cédric Pollet
Photographs copyright © Cédric Pollet (except where specified above)
First published in the English language in 2017 by Frances Lincoln Ltd, an imprint of The Quarto Group
The Old Brewery, 6 Blundell Street,
London N7 9BH, United Kingdom
T (0) 20 7700 6700   F (0)20 7700 8066
www.QuartoKnows.com

© 2016 Les Éditions Ulmer — 24, rue de Mogador, 75009 Paris

Editor: Antoine Isambert — Design: Guillaume Duprat
Translation for the Frances Lincoln edition: Caroline Harbouri

Revised edition 2017

A catalogue record for this book is available from the British Library.

978-0-7112-3915-9
Printed and bound in China
9 8 7 6 5 4 3 2 1

Brimming with creative inspiration, how-to projects and useful information to enrich your everyday life, Quarto Knows is a favourite destination for those pursuing their interests and passions. Visit our site and dig deeper with our books into your area of interest: Quarto Creates, Quarto Cooks, Quarto Homes, Quarto Lives, Quarto Drives, Quarto Explores, Quarto Gifts, or Quarto Kids.